£3

SI/220

Scrabble
A Chadian Childhood

World Writing in French
A Winthrop-King Institute Series

There is a growing interest among Anglophone readers in literature in translation, including contemporary writing in French in its richness and diversity. The aim of this new series is to publish cutting-edge contemporary French-language fiction, travel writing, essays and other prose works translated for an English-speaking audience. Works selected will reflect the diversity, dynamism, originality, and relevance of new and recent writing in French from across the archipelagoes – literal and figurative – of the French-speaking world. The series will function as a vital reference point in the area of contemporary French-language prose in English translation. It will draw on the expertise of its editors and advisory board to seek out and make available for English-language readers a broad range of exciting new work originally published in French.

To Amaboua

To the animals,
To the sick,
To the maimed

Mai ici commencent d'incorrigibles vivants

Sony Labou Tansi, *Ici commence ici*

Prelude

Very slowly, the child tilts his hand towards the shadows. The garden warblers have fallen silent and the song of the savannah bateleurs has faded. All you can hear is the shrill cry of the black widows, a dry grinding sound, the rattling of seeds, the crackling of insects. In the sky circle tawny-shaded eagles. They are powerful predators: their beaks are yellow with black tips.

In the courtyard, two children are playing, sitting face to face across a wooden table. The game consists of forming intersecting words on a grid with letters of different values. The score for letters or words is multiplied by two or three (double-letter score, triple-letter score, double-word score, triple-word score) according to the color of the squares: light blue or dark blue, salmon pink or baby pink, cherry red or blood red. Each player draws a letter, the one who gets closest to A will start the game.

The child reaches for the bag. It is a soft canvas bag the size of a hand, olive green, stitched on the sides and tied with a black cord. What will he find at the bottom of this dark pouch? He hears the flapping of the bedsheet drying, its light-colored fabric fluttering in the trade winds. Where does the wind go? Where does it come from? It is the wind that makes the sheets vibrate. The cord slides like a lace and the bag opens. Slowly, concentrating intently, he plunges his hand into the darkness.

Where are we, in what time, what is happening? The scene looks like a simple family game, and yet it holds something enigmatic that is almost imperceptible at first glance, but that grows the more you look at it—and the more you dwell on it, the bigger it gets. Beside the table, a woman observes the children: very beautiful, with an extraordinarily concerned air about her. The line of her eyebrows, fine but frowning, contrasts with the deceptive tranquility of the palm trees in the background. It is very hot—a glimmer of gold on a metal roof indicates where the sun strikes, and gives a sense of shellfire heat—but she is wearing big boots and a coat, as if she were preparing to leave. On the games table, an open medicine box (an unfolded leaflet, a ripped box showing two white tablets in a torn aluminum package) seems at odds with this snapshot of play and domesticity. And what are all of these raptors doing in the air, white-headed vultures, brown hawks with black spots, slate-colored hawks, birds of prey with their shrill lexicon (you can hear their raucous whistling now and their nonstop howling) that soar above, drawing circles in the sky?

This whole scene, as motionless as a still life, where all movement seems frozen in anticipation of the blow that is about to be delivered, but whose meaning remains unknown for the time being, is as captivating as a rebus and, like a rebus, is indecipherable. Its every detail is meticulously calculated, with admirable thoroughness and precision, but the overall composition remains mysteriously illegible. There is, so to speak, a shadow over the scene. It is as if we had entered into a suspended time and a forbidden zone.

The children themselves seem to be frozen in a falsely natural pose: they are not playing as normal, not as they do, not in that stubborn, heady, obstinate way, leaning over the table as if they were hanging over an abyss. Why are they playing? What are they playing? Strangely, and contradictorily, they seem simultaneously attentive and anesthetized, tense and inert, engaged and indifferent. Petrified by the importance of a game in which they are the protagonists but of which they understand neither the aims, nor the stakes, nor even how it is playing out. Sitting motionless, dumbfounded, they gravely contemplate the board, as if trying to discover its secret.

Soon, the words they exchange will do battle in the clouds. From a single line on the board, they will open up a great multitude of words and meanings, senses and significations, that travel deep and wide and far across time and space in waves that rise from the permutations of the letters and their position on the grid. From a few fixed points wrenched from the table and a few random letters drawn from the deep darkness, they will form words chosen for their value more than for their definition, which will carry with them an incredibly wide range of brainwaves and palpitations: intonations and inflections, onomatopoeias and tonalities, phonemes and phenomena, quivers and vibrations. Horizontally, vertically, a palette of beasts, people, and spirits will fall into place, halfway between truth and terror, making incisions on the bark, cracking the wood, piercing the table and sometimes lifting it up, pulling along in their wake all the whirlwinds of meaning and the giddiness of the voice, expanding the sensations and driving them away from the abyss—or, ultimately, driving them back to it.

But for now the vultures—and all the other birds of prey scrambling for the pickings—make heard their grunts that sound like those of pigs fighting around a carcass. Already, the shrieking yellow-throated sentries have reached the dark densities of the ivy that hangs from the corner of the old wall eaten by the sun, then they fall silent for good. There is total silence now. Deadly silence. We remain there motionless, sad, and knowing, between dance and combat.

*

The war was approaching but we didn't know it. It always comes in like that, in small steps. It is a she-wolf who has lost her young and who is ready to do anything to eat. The wolf's gait is distinctive: supple, fluid, flexible. A succession of strides balanced on the tips of its toes. Quite quick, but above all with great endurance. Its prey may well shake it off for a while, but it will eventually catch them. Its mouth is open, jutting forward, the ears point backwards. She never seems to get tired. War moves in the same way, advancing in a slow trot, but always ends up devouring you.

Soldiers. Soldiers marching in the dust. They are young, very young, and in some cases almost as young as me. I am ten years old. I see them pass. Turbaned, with their eyes hidden behind sunglasses, they march along the sidewalks, dragging their rifles in a train of dust, gather in their dozens round an armored car in the middle of a crossroads or rush like a whirlwind onto the cargo bed of a pickup truck with its radiator grill torn off, its sides streaked with large orange sand marks.

In town, they are everywhere. We see them on guard outside the gate of the Camp of April 13, figures standing very straight in front of the whitewashed walls, black statues on a white background. Dignified and upright when they are on guard at the doors of official buildings, near the football stadium you find them sitting, legs dangling, their rifles on their upper thighs, their pistols loosely slipped into their belts as they sit on the bar terraces. They are irresistibly drawn to the roundabouts: they meet up there squatting, Kalashnikovs between their knees, holding the breech firmly but playing with the barrel, turning it between their fingers. There is always something not quite right with their uniforms, combat pants that are a little too short or a little too big, a cartridge belt that is badly strapped, mismatched boots, a knife sticking out of its sheath and threatening to fall to the ground.

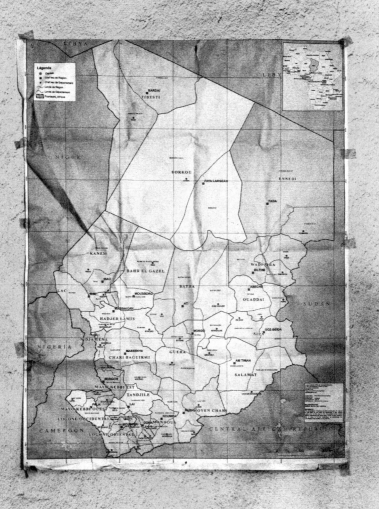

Scrabble

*

We are in N'Djamena, in February 1979. N'Djamena was first called Fort-Lamy, during colonial times, in tribute to a commander of the French army who died in combat a few weeks before the city was founded: it is a *martial* city. Chad is ruled by General Félix Malloum. He is facing a rebellion from the north, led by Goukouni Oueddeï, supported behind the scenes by the Libya of General Gaddafi. Everyone has their finger on the trigger.

On February 12, 1979, the first fighting broke out in the capital. This is what has sometimes been called the "first N'Djamena war." This fighting—and all others that followed—was accompanied by diverse forms of violence, looting, hostage-taking, various kinds of torture and massacres of civilians.

*

Here I am now, on high in the tree of seasons. Now I withdraw to the other side from the sun and summon up dense and obscure things of the past. Little by little, memory comes back. I see myself again in the courtyard, sitting with my brother with the letters and lines before us, weighing each word to know where to place it and to increase its score. The Indian apple plant has white flowers and thorns, it is a powerful drug that is given to the sick or the condemned, pregnant women or prisoners who are going to be executed. It allows them to stay calm and to forget things.

But when I close my eyes, I first fall as if drowning into the muddy waters of the Chari river, which traces the border between Chad and Cameroon, and into which so many men, women, and even children were thrown, sometimes still alive, their hands knotted behind their backs, or tied up in a shoulder bag. I sink with them towards the sand and the clay, down amidst the green and the brown, passing purple weeds, shards of pottery, and crocodile scales. My head is heavier than a cannonball and carries me towards the abyss: I dive into a bottomless bag where the letters collide or slip away, call out to or ignore each other, I bathe in an unlimited space free from the constraints of cycles and dates, and I enter into the time of childhood, which indeed has no concept of time.

Then I hear the tumult of the years hurtling by in my skull like herds of Kouri cattle, their muzzles held high, their long, broad ears, their horns sticking out, countless jackals hanging onto their throats. The bulls roar, move from island to island in the reeds of the lake and swim freely: as soon as their hooves touch the black clay, they gain a foothold and begin a fabulous *ascent*, passing through the centuries and carrying me away like a hummingbird on their back. At other times, they are zebus with mahogany hair and lyre-shaped horns. When I leave with them in my dream, the river no longer scares me, I sail all night on their necks, going upstream towards the source. I feel the cadence beating in my head, in perfect time: the dream and the rhythm go together, they do not separate. Their slow but sure pace, on the edge between the land and the water, opens up some old landscapes inside of me: all my memories take flight in the desert wind, the past flows down the river, plays out in the branches, explodes in the foliage. The past is all around me now—and I laugh when I say "the past," because none of all this is past.

Thus, my childhood opens up like a mango: I see again the sunny mornings quiver in a sparkle of details, the jagged lace of the leaves and branches, the earth shiny with having been swept so much, the red and yellow pepper plants, and the peaceful whiteness of the walls. I hear my mother's voice, a sound deep like water ("Come on, it's your turn to play ..."), all through the shady afternoons spent sheltering under the veranda roof. In the evening, which shivers with the yellow glow of the lamps and the trails of black fumes rising from the zinc lanterns, I gather a handful of memories hanging from the large green leaves of the banana trees, I collect the sounds and the scents, seizing them as they fly on the wind. At dusk, I find myself in the company of the lengthening shadows that prepare the pepper, the corn, and the fish in the smell of burnt charcoal, the laughter that rises up and the crackling of the wood.

The first player shuffles the letters in the bag and draws the initial seven. The pieces are taken one by one from the dark pouch and placed face down on the table. They are perfectly smooth, square, in lightly painted wood. The letters and their values (A1, B2, C2 ... M3, K10, L1, F4 ...) are written in black on an ivory background. They bear no distinctive sign: it is an alphabet of finely printed letters and simple figures. But the child, from these few luminous and unassuming letters, already sees emerging unfamiliar words, sonorous discoveries, unexpected meanings. From this meager wooden booty, he will soon raise a forest of very ancient signs mixed with new characters, whose lineage enchants him and whose range delights him. And everything, absolutely everything that will be recounted now, will be told from this power of childhood, from these few pieces of wood arranged on the table, and from a starry central square on which the first word played will be placed.

TOUMAÏ

1

I had a childhood of sand and dust. Life had placed us there, without any warning, between the savannah and the steppe.

Chad, for me, is first and foremost the wind. The sound of the wind. The dog attached to the stake by his leash so that it can't devour the hens pecking in the yard goes mad because of the wind. His eyes sting and his ears itch; he is slowly eroded by the wind. Little by little, he himself becomes completely gray like the dust. It is a land of gravel and rage.

Later, long after the events I am now about to recount, I will look at a map in an atlas and understand everything. In this country closed like a gourd, without access to the sea and surrounded by other countries that are at once neighbors and enemies (Libya, Niger, Nigeria, Cameroon, Central African Republic, Sudan), the wind is both a shiver that circulates, the bearer of good and bad news, and the perceptible breath of time, which brings everything and takes everything away. As it rises, so do the rains and fire, life and death, war and song.

I had a childhood of sand and dust.

Later, I will read in books that the Bodélé Depression, a little farther north, is the place in the world with the most dust. When it blows between the rocky massifs of Ennedi and Tibesti, it creates the principal source of dust on Earth, a very light, porous, crumbly silica whose color veers from light gray to blue-green according to the shape of the dunes and the time of day. Here, the wind has blown so constantly for millions of years that it has traced in the desert great corridors lined with rocky spurs that resemble the hulls of ships raised towards the sky, which are transformed in each moment by the subtle architecture of the wind.

But, for the moment, I am ten years old and I am discovering this dust carried by the wind, which seems to blow everywhere and not to settle anywhere. A powder that is by turns very red and very yellow, very fine and yet hard and painful on the skin, as if it were constantly crumbling from a clifftop. Sometimes the wind and the dust come together at once. This creates opal tornadoes with a light of almost unbearable whiteness. A sandstorm: the sky turns yellow, the winds howl and blow in all directions. It's the most vivid picture you can paint yourself of chaos.

The wind also has its beauty, which gradually reveals itself. When it caresses the treetops, the upturned leaves reveal several shades of silver, pink, or cream. From time to time, at the slightest breath of air, when flocks of chirping birds fly free from the branches, emerald-green petals settle on the paths. I realize that the wind is not just an unbounded horseman scraping the corrugated iron rooftops. It also reveals, when it ruffles the carpet of tall grasses as it blows through them, the stubble of sorghum with its flag-shaped leaves and, behind the plots of shiny-leaved shrubs, it shakes before my eyes the crimson of the flamboyant tree, the bright, vivid yellow of an acacia on the savannah, the pink-and-red pods of the golden rain tree.

From sunrise to sunset, I observe the play of light, approaching, appearing, flowing then disappearing, flowing back, and disappearing. From time to time, it fades to the point of extinction and suddenly, just before dying in the fiery evening, reignites—and it is white, pink, gold, and silver, with such a radiance that, arising yet from the same forms, unexpected colors constantly come to life. Like, from a few wooden counters on a Scrabble board, the unending efflorescence of known terms and strange or unexpected words.

On the terrace in front of the house, before my mother calls us for dinner, I wait for this spectacle every evening, I see it coming: then the whole world is in the grip of a great upheaval. The shadows rise from all around, everywhere the clouds open, the colors rush in. The squawking birds escape towards the river, the men slip away into their huts, the dogs howl at the night. It is a complete catastrophe of colors and sounds: in the distance, cautious, worried, a final few passers-by hurry across the bridge. All kinds of shades escape from the battle of the sunset on the wooded slopes and the reflection of the waters: smoky, reddish orange tones, bruised pinks .... Then, when darkness sets across the land of humankind, the songs rise from the huts and are now alone against the night—and every day, at the same time, while the child looks out from the terrace, his eyes wide open and all his senses inured, the miracle occurs.

Childhood is the age of questions. I asked an uncommon number of them.

Why are some ants red? And others black?

Why is the lizard green and how can the chameleon change color? Why does the dragonfly have four wings and the butterfly only two? How is it that the turtle is so slow and the gecko so fast?

Why does the wind sometimes rise up and other times go down?

Where does all this sand come from?

What is rain?

Or else: Why do sugar and salt, which are both white, taste so different? How can you explain that the leaf of the neem tree is so smooth and that of the fig tree so rough?

Why is the roar of the zebu deep and long, while that of the ox which has no hump is shorter and shriller?

How is it that we can be hot and cold at the same time?

Then, with age, my questions become more precise but also more abstract. One day I find myself in front of a hollow tree trunk covered by a palm leaf, around which bees are buzzing: why is the newly made honey whiter than the old honey? And when my father gives me a watch for my birthday: why do the hands turn from left to right and from top to bottom? What is time? And what if it didn't exist?

As a child, I always had a finger in my mouth. Even at ten, I still eat everything, or more exactly I *taste*. Everything that comes to hand, I scrutinize it bit by bit, I smell it then I feel it, I throw it away, or I swallow it. All day spent foraging, my butt in the grasses and my hands in the ground: I grope and I find, I pluck and I ferret out, I shove things in and spit them back out. I learn about the sands and their depths. I find three coins on my way, I munch on them immediately: they are dry and hard with a slightly acid taste. Plantains are less sweet than pink bananas; I devour them both. I gobble flies and even wasps. I graze like a buffalo. I know the taste of herbs and leaves by heart: couch grass is sweet and refreshing, dayflower viscous and a little bitter, lemongrass pleasant and tangy. As for the earth, it is grainy and salty: I know it, I have eaten it. I get to know the immense multitude of things by their shape, their color, their smell, their flavor, but also by their texture and, so to speak, their *complexion*.

I also learn to listen. The sonic ambiance, the sounds of the body and those of nature. Starting early in the morning, from the nearby mosque, the muezzin calls to prayer. From the top of the spherical dome, his nomadic voice is cast into the emptiness and reverberates throughout the city, all along the white walls, while the faithful bow their heads to the ground. It is not the horn of the Jews nor the bell of the Christians: it is a human voice. It was in Chad that I first experienced the power of the voice.

And then there are still more immense noises, or little, thin sounds, a whole strange and incomprehensible theory of music, to which you have to listen patiently to make of it an ally. It's a sonic gold mine, a store of noise for life. I still hear them today. The humming of insects (clouds of flies during the day, swarms of mosquitoes at night). The first cry of the teals, slightly shrill and creaky, which rises just before the sun. Soon there will be hundreds of them, and the bush will be nothing more than a long crackling sound. In the trees along the river, the red-faced Gambian geese wake up and start to hiss. All around, the world utters its cry.

*

From afar.

Greenery, whiteness, sand.

Simply emblazoned, always renewed.

However, as soon as you move closer and pay attention to it …

Knowledge through the soil, on the tip of your heel, by the palm of your hand. If I spend my nights contemplating the sky, my head in the stars, I spend my days bent over, my nose in the undergrowth. Whether on flat, bare ground or, on the contrary, ground with bushy wild grasses, all the fantastic punctuation of the earth appears to me. The variety of pebbles and stones, like flint full stops on the clay or dewdrops; the commas of grasses scattered over the mud and the accents of various stems; the question marks of dasheen leaves; the accents and brackets of bramble branches; the parentheses formed by shaded arbors, covered with plants that seem to protect a secret; the quotation marks of a fern growing out of the sun at the bottom of a crack in the rock and whose leaves close when you touch them. It's a whole gravel of grammar, a euphoria of signs infinitely restarting, which I never grow tired of.

I lean over the mysteries. I adopt a way of looking that skims over things, precise like a scalpel—a lateral, informed vision, right up close to things. Concentrated. Affectionate, one might say. In the midst of a collective blindness, that of grown-ups, the position at ground level—that of the sniper—does not only provide extraordinarily rich and poetically precise material. It also brings a vertical break in sensation: thanks to it, childhood helps us to see the appearance of the world in full light.

Even as I grow up, I never give up on it altogether, and I keep the habit of living bent over. Still today, and everyone is surprised by it, it often happens that my body is abnormally bent over in the photographs that are taken of me. It's my look, it's a habit. It comes to me from childhood.

So, I see all the clay and water, mud and sand. At ground level, where I find myself, everything crackles and takes on a singular relief, a startling force. Each speck of dust becomes a map of the world. Even better, the most varied scales overlap or intersect with each other. There are impenetrable scrubs, fences with no way through, bushes even a snake could not slide through. And then there are shrubs, tufts, and rocks that cats cross, where lizards dance and birds come to play.

It is life at ground level: I share it with the animals. Very quickly, I make the acquaintance of the loud, pot-bellied, rough-skinned cane toad, which sings after heavy rain. I sometimes come across the very timid little multicolored frog, which is so beautiful but sinks into the sand as soon as you approach it. A shy creature. I observe the red ants, which are very small but whose bite causes a terrible burning sensation. Nasty little guys. I become friends with amphibians, mollusks, insects, and crabs. I fight over fruits with the birds and the ants. But I am wary of the scorpion and do not seek a quarrel with him. I quickly realize that all these animals are both wild and incredibly intelligent. Their simultaneous strength and vulnerability touch me. I train myself to be attentive to this fragility.

Soon, I become bolder: I speak with the doves and I chat with the beetles. I sympathize with the wild puppies that come to prowl in the rose bushes in search of food and little red sparrows. I am also familiar with the immense population of locusts: there are the blue locusts, the red locusts, the black locusts with a creamy belly decorated with black dots, the earth-colored locusts, and the fire-colored locusts. To really know the world, I realize that you have to learn everything, take everything in: the shape, the colors, the smells, the texture, the dimensions, the landscape, the distances …. And that even if you do this, it is still more beautiful, more terrifying, and more varied than you think.

In the thickets and undergrowth, I search for the rhythm of the light, between the swaying foliage, the tip of a branch that pokes your eye and some smoke rising into the sky. There are several kinds of lights: some can be bright and fleeting, others compact and abundant, lush. Still others are deep and tender. From time to time, they meet up and play together. Sometimes they combine—and sometimes, on the contrary, they diverge only to find themselves immediately parts of a dazzling fan, a glimmering iridescence. I get up and in front of me, in the distance, is the exclamation mark of a palm tree.

Very quickly, too, I go from the ground to the sky, I flip my head back and I find myself up high. You have to be on the lookout, to be listening out. I try to follow all the rustling, the rattling, the whistles that rise up from the ground and scatter into the air, refrains, phrasings, songs. I myself am a little man, a tiny shape posed at random in the great din of the universe, but by following the tracks of ants on the trunks of trees or those of the white storks as they take flight, their legs elongated, their wings spread, their beaks open in the splendor of the evening—that's what childhood is, the smallest detail can carry you very far—I feel connected to all of the world's murmurings.

2

The bag passes to the opponent and the board swivels. In drawing the letters, the players have different strategies. Some people place the pouch at eye level so that none of the other players can see the letters in the bag; others hesitate for a long time, feeling around with their fingers and nails, weighing each wooden piece and throwing furtive sideways glances; others still plunge their hands into the bag with a resolute gesture and, as if they intended to extract from it a decisive secret that has been too long concealed, go boldly to seek out the engraved tiles in the very depths of the darkness.

The board turns and I see the whole scene again. A strange blend of very slow and almost infinitely decomposed sequences (the backs, the players' shoulders, their faces which are hidden as my vision passes across them from the right, their smiles now almost erased) and very short, quick, fragmented sequences: a hand falling to the table to pick up a letter, a glimpse of the courtyard through the green-and-black thickness of the banana trees, the wing of an airplane in the sky, a pen scribbling a mark on a sheet of paper.

From these cut-up images, a delicate and light prose, a weaving of composite elements each time wonderfully arranged, it is difficult to recapture its full scale, to measure its full complexity. What meaning will emerge later from these almost offhand contests which nevertheless seem strangely desperate? For the moment, I am trying to reconstitute a territory, a garden, fruit trees. I can see the leaves and assess the shadows. I recognize the line of the river in the distance, the canoes speak to me, I imagine that they carry fish and nets, I myself go back up the rivers in my dreams, I cross the tributaries and the holes filled with standing water, and I bring back in my nets the magic spells of childhood.

Now the house is coming back to me and I'm starting to understand. I see again the lock fixed on the left side of the door, the iron-teethed key on which also hung a padlock. The door opens to the outside, the living room is clean and bright, a bouquet of hibiscus stands out, a purple spot on the white wall, like a discreet sign of encouragement. The kitchen is farther away, with its light tiling, the clinking of cups and spoons, the throbbing of the refrigerator, the scent of wine in the jars and the smell of charcoal.

I retrace my steps and take the corridor towards the bedrooms. What is at the other end of this corridor full of shade and sunlight? Memories scatter—a breach in the ceiling, a ripped-out floor—then come together in clusters. In the recesses of the corridor remain some areas of mystery: why these holes in the walls and these shattered windows? Life had thrown us there between the desert and the people. Under my parents' bed, there is a large chasm that opens up. The windows rattle, the curtains are torn. The wind blows scents of powder and grilled meat into the room.

I sit in the corner of a cupboard. Dry cracking sounds—the sheets blowing in the wind and sun no doubt—and I see the bursts of color fluttering over my skin. I hear the roar of the large birds that pass by, not very far above my head. From one room to another, memory comes back, forcefully now .... Inside of me, in this great palace of my memory, the sky, the earth, the savannah and the desert, the bush, the cities and the streets, and all that I could have noticed there, the men, the beasts, and the howling are revealed to me whenever I want, except for the things that I have forgotten. But all the rooms are reopened in the immense palace of my memory, and I have not forgotten anything.

*

My father was quite dark-skinned and my mother very white. Between his café-au-lait color and her lily tint, I found an astonishing harmony, a concordance, which was precisely that of my birth. In almost every other way, they were different, or rather they complemented each other in a strange way. Birds of a feather flock together, as the saying goes. But so far as they were concerned, their marriage was rather the coupling of two exceptional singularities, which made their very differences the cement that bonded their complicity. Their union lasted more than fifty years, until the death of my mother. In a certain way, it endures still.

Scrabble

My father is a soldier. He enlisted at a very young age and spent his entire career in the army, which allowed him to escape poverty and start a family. He believes in order, in authority, in respecting the word given and the oath taken. He also has a tremendous critical spirit and a caustic sense of humor, which will earn him some enmity. He hates verbiage and always has good-humored people on his side. He has a curious mixture of insolence and loyalty, as is sometimes found in the French army.

He has his hands full with his two sons. He often turns up to pull us by the ears and give us a clout. For no good reason, he gives my brother and me some memorable hidings. An untidy room, and it's a torrent of blows that rain down on our heads, our thighs, our shoulders, our buttocks. A broken glass, a volley of slaps on the cheeks. A poor grade, a battery of slaps and whacks. He doesn't really hurt us—he taps with the edge of the hand and never closes his fist—but he still hits us often, with energy, humor, and delight. His specialty: correcting us several times for the same fault, according to an unchanging pattern that we will learn to fear as well as to mock, my brother and I. First, there is an intense distribution of slaps, a rain of clouts and smacks: a real downpour. Then it's the lull. We think that the worst is over, but during this time he ruminates, he broods, he ponders .... His memory turns in loops recalling our villainy, the full extent of our vexations .... Second passage, like a squadron of mirages: a carpet-bombing of clouts diving down upon us, a bombardment of slaps. He chases us through the house, shouting, I break into terrible sprints—he comes back a few minutes later, when you thought the issue was over, only to shoot us down again: I become prodigiously hardy. Thus, I work on both my speed and my resistance. But, as he says, it's for my own good: also, the more he tears my hair out, the more he slaps me, the more I am convinced that he is an excellent father and that I am an ungrateful child. Still today, with one last remnant of caution and a touch of irony, I have not really changed my mind.

My mother is sweetness itself. Her skin, her gestures, her voice: everything about her is soft, caressing, and full of tenderness, melodious like honey, affectionate to the point of savagery. No soppiness, however: very possessive, like many people from a disadvantaged background, she retains something bitter in her very benevolence and, beneath the silky touch of her manners, a hint of violence in her way of loving.

Bougainvilleas are her favorite plants. It gives purple or pink, orange or white flowers, delicate and violent in her image. They are everywhere on the terrace, in the hedges, over the low walls, hung at the corner of the walls and climbing up to the rooftops. As soon as a ray of sunshine appears, the bougainvilleas light up. The shape of the flowers becomes more intense and their color more vivid, their outline is imbued with a particular vibration. Each grove becomes a palace of light in the bushy branches. Even today, as soon as I see one, flaming and red in the shade of a path, I think I see my mother coming towards me, delicate and radiant, and throwing me her clear look, floral and dazzling, from the top of its branches.

Finally, there is my brother. Régis is two years older than me. As is often the case with brothers, Régis and I are like chalk and cheese. I like books and music, he prefers tools and making things. I am terribly clumsy, he is very clever with his hands. I wear great big spectacles, he has very good eyesight. I never say a word, he never stops moaning and muttering. And in spite of all these differences, he never reprimands me, always stands by my side and defends me against the whole world: that is what you call a brother, I would say.

*

All around the house is the courtyard. The yard is more than my world: it is my kingdom.

It is quite large, rectangular in shape and fenced off with upright and thorny wood. Since my mother has been taking care of it, it has come to be covered with trees and plants: it is a profusion of flowers, dominated by the multiple yellow and white notes of the cotton plants on the red flushes of the flamboyant trees. Around the house, there are many creepers, which attract the monkeys: it is not uncommon to see them doing acrobatics above the house, among the yellow flowers and blue-necked larks.

During the day, everything is organized around the yard: play, work, animal rearing, trade, cooking, washing, laundry, drying. In the evening: drinks, gossip. It's the pulsating heart of existence. In the morning, a goat is milked, the pigs are given cassava peelings, and there is grass for the rabbits in their hutches. At noon, the meat or fish is grilled and the vegetables boiled out the back, behind the house kitchen. In the afternoon, after a siesta on the terrace, in the sugary shade of a small gardenia, we play all kinds of games and contests: water fights, to cool off as much as to have fun, hunting for ants, fights, and running races with the young goats. Finally, in the evening, it's time for rest and stories. Life goes on like this, the yard empties and fills up, with people, noises, animals, fruit .... Because everything that comes in passes through the yard, everything that happens takes place in the yard: news, food, visitors and cars, sheep, cattle, humans, the final sighs of the evening and the first laughter of the morning.

And then, in a corner, there is the hut.

The hut: that is what everyone calls it. It has no other name. As if there were only one of them, one that is alike and yet not alike all other similar buildings. The hut is not round, or postern-shaped, like the ones I would see later in most books on Africa; it is rectangular. It is located on the side of the road, inside the yard, just next to the entrance gate. The walls are made of banco (raw earth bricks dried in the sun), the roof made of woven plants, there is neither water nor electricity. This is the caretaker's hut. It constitutes, so to speak, the border post between my universe and the outside world. The hut marks an impassable limit, the barrier to the new.

The caretaker himself, I will never know his name: he is a simple silhouette, a shadow cast on the walls, a ghost standing by the thorny hedge. Equipped with his large bunch of keys connected by a rope to the stitching of his djellaba, he monitors the comings and goings. He opens the gate, closes it, he does his rounds with unerring regularity. He deters thieves, keeps beggars away. I don't remember if he was skinny, fat, bald or hairy, young or very old. I don't remember his face, or even if he had one: for me, he was just a rustling of sleeves and a clatter of metal, who scared me out of my wits. But I remember that he was tall and that he lived in the hut, and that gave him a sort of terrible prestige.

Obviously, the hut attracts me irresistibly. It took me a long time to get into it. First, I approach it with cautious steps, I go around it, reluctant and sniffing, almost squeaking, like a puppy around its first prey. From the outside, you can see only the bricks of dried earth mixed with chopped straw. At night, these strands glisten in the clay like glitter, and this sparkling of tiny precious stones gives it an additional aura. Looking up, I can see very distinctly a framework of branches assembled with iron wire and crowned with superimposed bark rings, covered with a bed of palms. It's very simple and very beautiful: a subtle blend of basketry and pottery.

Little by little, I become bolder. I am afraid of the hut, but at the same time, I am captivated by its frontier presence. One day, I get very close to it. At the threshold, there is what the Chadians call a *tungulé*, a mound of earth placed at the entrance to prevent water from getting in during the rainy season, and this tiny little tongue of earth pointed like a stiletto, sharp and slightly rounded, is enough to prevent me from going in. To tell the truth, it terrifies me, as if it marked the entrance to a forbidden domain.

However, the door is open. By fearfully placing myself at an angle, stretching and twisting my neck like a chicken having its throat cut, I manage to peep inside. Taking a look into the hut is like looking inside a chasm. The hut is dark and deep: on the side, a single opening, without shutters, overlooks the yard and lets through a crack of light, which lights up absolutely nothing but, by contrast, brings into relief the radiant darkness. Lesson from the darkness: everything else is immersed in an impenetrable opacity, an inky blackness. The hut seems to be struck blind. Suddenly, above my head, hanging from the door frame, I notice a huge gray spiderweb in which flies are wriggling and, on a thread, a camel spider as big as a hand coming towards me. At the same time, I hear, coming from inside the hut, murmurs and then a cascade of voices. Terrified, I run away.

*

"We have to start from a principle." I often hear this phrase in the mouth of adults, spoken in a definitive tone and accompanied by a peremptory gesture. This expression fascinates me. I never start from a principle, I don't even know what it is. I always start from what I have to hand or before my eyes at a given moment: a blade of grass growing, a root tearing out from the ground, a winding trickle of water. All the work of the earth and its depths, this obscure secretion which gives birth to worlds. A crawling ant, a leaping cricket. A blue-winged dragonfly taking flight in the sunshine …. If that is a principle, so much the better.

I have no toys, or very few. On the other hand, I like all ball games, football, table tennis, hoop racing, spinning tops, marbles …. Anything round, slender, that slides, everything that rolls and bounces, that moves infinitely.

But what catches my attention, what interests me above all, is people. They come by, alone or in small groups, throwing up clouds of fine dust in their wake. Shepherds, travelers, traders. Farmers, fishermen, merchants. At any time of day, they crowd around in front of the yard to sell or trade something. A man stands at the gate: he carries a lamb on his shoulders. The caretaker lets him in. Frilly sleeves and keys flow over his hips. The man makes his way across the yard. He will come out a few minutes later, counting his banknotes, and with three live chickens taken from their cages, their legs tied by a cord and cackling warily, their heads hanging down along his left leg.

Occasionally, workers come to repair an engine or a roof, a window. They lay things out, they calculate, they measure, they organize. In rhythm, they pound, they circle, they weed. Sometimes I catch sight of a scar on the face of a mechanic, or the wrinkled hands of a basket maker. I admire their physical force, a little unsettling for a ten-year-old child, and their technique, which can be applied equally well to working wood, iron, glass, or sand …. In the evening, artists approach the hut to sell their creations: my mother always welcomes them with open arms. She barters vigorously (and with a hint of amusement), but always ends up paying them a good price. Huge tapestries in particular, wider than they are long, full of color, with a touch of humor or poetry: a few seashells or a bird's beak. I look at them over and again, these tapestries: those with reptiles, it looks like they are crawling, those with bird wings, it looks like they are going to fly away.

I still cannot explain it, even if I already understand it intuitively: these artists and these workers, so skillful in their know-how and so elegant in their ingenuity, are custodians not only of a trade and a technique but above all of a formidable life force. It is this phenomenal vitality that carries them on roofs or in the trees (like birds), or else in mud and in the ground (like snakes), leaves or scrap metal (like tortoises or like dogs), and forges with their hands works that are as useful as they are beautiful.

Observing the relationship between adults takes up a big part of my day. My appetite for foreign languages is born here, in the accents and phonemes of lexicons that I do not know, and whose meanings and nuances I gradually learn to guess. What does this word mean? This gesture? How to respond to these kinds of questions? It takes a constant effort of *translation*. In Arabic, in French, in Hausa, in Musey, it is a space with several triggers, to be discovered with every sentence, its heterogeneity, its polyphony.

I especially like the greetings that the workers launch into joyfully, delighted to have been paid, or the artists overwhelmed by my mother's generosity.

"Be well! Be alive, goodbye, may you all be in good health, do not stumble along the way ...."

"If you go by pirogue, arrive safely to shore; if you go by camel, let the dunes carry you!"

These are expressions of politeness that resonate in the air long after the gate has closed, and which always express not the hope but the need to see each other again. And, even though this reunion with the house of my childhood is now impossible, I hear them today more keenly than ever.

When evening finally comes, a fire is lit, around which everyone gathers, their bellies turned towards the flame. To earn more money at month's end, the caretaker sells cigarettes in front of his hut. The shadows pass back and forth across the oil lamp. Packages pass from hand to hand. Sudden gusts of wind blow through the bushes causing puffs of smoke and sparks to rise, which for an instant light up more vividly the beautiful black hands with their blue nails. The caretaker digs into the embers and turns over the red charcoal under the cauldron in which a large piece of white fish is cooking in boiling water. Everyone's eyes are fixed on the fire.

For large festive ceremonies, a sheep is dragged by a rope, tied up, and its throat slit. Its wool is soft and warm, its flanks quiver and its eyes are frightened. Its neck is soft and curly-haired. Songs rumble to the beat of tom-toms or are chanted to the rhythm of calabash shells. The caretaker approaches the animal and holds it tightly to himself for a long time, stroking its spine. You can tell he loves his sheep, that he wishes it no harm. He paid quite a lot for it, after all. He whispers prayers while sharpening his knife. Suddenly the white blade flashes in the glow of the flames. Then, very quickly, he cuts its throat, taking care that the muzzle is facing Mecca. The animal moves, its legs tremble, it goes into convulsions. It widens its eyes to seize for a moment more the secret of its life.

Then its gaze falls and its head swirls before tumbling downwards. Still held firmly by the caretaker's arm, in successive hiccups, the blood empties from his body.

Then the songs of the long night come back to my memory, I see the two infinite eyes of the child that look avidly into the darkness, and the hut itself becomes a little ball of night in the night, and time itself collapses into the night.

3

He was called Baba Saleh. I never knew if that was his real name. At that time, the servants didn't really have a name—and then the Chadian names were a bit too complicated, as white people would say, so just call him Saleh. Baba Saleh at least, it was easy to remember, especially for a cook. A salty baba! I asked him: he had never eaten it. So, think about it: flour, baker's yeast, brioche dough! And a Polish inventor …. The taunts of the European children over his name left him cold. I learned later that Saleh was a family name and Baba a first name. But I never heard anyone call him anything other than "Saleh." Or else: "the boy."

Saleh was a *boy*, that is to say someone who did a bit of everything: a domestic worker, an employee of the house. A servant. *Boy* is also the name of a very gentle little bird that makes its nest in yam wood, but that was not what people were thinking of when they called him "the boy."

Saleh was robust and vigorous: he looked like a mason who had just cemented a wall or a carpenter having finished a formwork. He was tall, well built, his chest bulging, but his legs were thinner than the rest of his body, which gave him an effeminate air and a certain grace. In addition, he walked with a slight sway: his right knee was unstable and a tiny but noticeable rolling movement enlivened the dance-like way he walked. Some said that his kneecap had been riddled by the shrapnel from a mine nestled under the sand when he lived in the north of the country (the Tibesti and the Borkou are riddled with mines), before migrating to the capital to flee the advance of the rebellion. Others said that he fell from a roof when he was a carpenter and had to look for a new job. In any case, the contrast between his fragile legs and his powerful chest gave the impression of someone who had to fight to make his way, who had done it all by himself, pulling himself out of the clay to hoist himself towards the surface, the legacy of which was a vaguely disturbing physical deformation that nevertheless gave him his charm. He was a cripple with a hint of elegance, a lame man on his way to the dance.

*

Saleh is tireless. He takes care of the shopping, cleaning, meals, the garden, laundry, and dishes. As he spends a lot of time in the yard under the blazing sun, his skin is always shiny, traversed by yellow and white flashes that trace tattoos of light on his beautiful black body. He always wears the same gray tank top with dark red stripes, white shorts that remain mysteriously clean as he carries out all his tasks and whose brightness helps to identify him from afar, while he moves ceaselessly from the washhouse to the kitchen, from the kitchen to the poultry yard and from the poultry yard to the clothesline.

Saleh can do everything: he brushes the ironwork, fixes the straw, clears the mud, hangs the skins, then, having fed the animals and done the grocery shopping as he skips along with his dancing gait, prepares lunch by scraping the wheat flours, kneads the semolina in the company of the caretaker's wives who gently make fun of him, his eternal undershirt stuck to his chest and back with perspiration. Saleh can do everything, but his specialty is cooking. As soon as he can escape from the household chores, he spends most of his time at the back of the garden, near the chicken coop and the rabbit cages where wood, charcoal, and the food he brings back from the market are piled up on the brown earth floor. There, near the trampled ash of the previous day's fire, accumulate sorghum, corn, millet, and black-eyed peas, stored in plastic bags, metal containers, pots, or jars. And tons of fruit, heaped ears of corn to be beaten, huge amounts of pulses, powders, pastes, liquids ... and sometimes even a fillet of wild antelope drying in the sun.

The kitchen is right next door: you enter it through a somewhat rickety screened service door placed above a large worn rock that acts as a stairway. This is where Saleh prepares the meals that he will delight us with: earthenware jars of manioc, of flour and salt, of red sorghum and white sorghum, as well as the pearl millet that is used in all his sauces: garlic, okra, dried peppers, cinnamon and cloves, honey, corn and peanuts …. Grilled fish, especially captain fish, served with peppers and ginger. More rarely, tender kouri beef with parsley, porcupine meat, or a tasty gazelle, eaten with rice, tomatoes, and onions.

Saleh commands the forces of nature: the iron of the cauldron whose sides he drums with an oxtail rubbed with spices and a bunch of carrots, the fire that he fans or extinguishes with a single gesture of his hand, the puffs of steam above the pot through which his round face emerges smiling at me. But he is also a great teacher: he knows all the plants and their uses by heart, trees and seeds, superstitions and divinations. He will teach me over the years about the herbs, dried, pounded, or ground in a shard of pottery, marinated in a can of palm wine, and samples of roots that are gently sucked to ward off disease. He will teach me the traps for all kinds of animals (*gombi* for small birds, *goni* for large animals): the drop trap, snare trap or snap trap, slip knots, nets, to catch squirrels, pigeons, red larks, guinea fowl …. As I grow up, he will introduce me to the rites used to ward off evil spirits: what the Kanouris call the "work of the hand," occult techniques, magnetic passes, protection spells, incantations. The hand must be both flexible and firm, the fingers agile, the body straining towards the gesture and the mind towards the target. Even today, I don't write in any other way. Thanks to him, I become the master of traps, a specialist in bewitchments.

When Saleh is working, he is extraordinarily calm, composed, methodical. He fulfills his many tasks meticulously. But when he explains things, he becomes excited, intoxicating. His gait, already sprightly with his slight limp, becomes light and bouncing. His arms windmill the air and his big feet kick up the dust in a clatter of worn-out shoes, his voice carried like a drum across the sands of the desert. His body is a cascade of gestures, from his mouth springs a torrent of magic formulas, proclaimed very loudly and very slowly or, quite the opposite, whispered to a frenetic rhythm, between allegory and muttering.

There flow from Saleh's mouth endless extraordinary stories: often, when night falls, he takes my brother and me to the side of the hut to tell us a story in his own style. He hums: "My blue-eyed brothers, sit down … my silver-hipped sisters, sit down …." Everyone circles around him. The little girl and the hyena, the little boy and the lion, the princess eaten by the crocodile, the monkey and the caiman, the saga of the king of the dogs …. For years, he will shower us with legends, a different one for each evening, by the light of the kerosene lamp and in all the richness of the shadows that covered our faces.

One of them, for example, has stayed in my memory:

"A ram, a dog and a small bird want to go near the town of Sarh, on the border between Chad and Cameroon. A truck stops: it's a bush taxi. The ram asks:

'How much is it to go to the border?'

'Five hundred CFA francs,' replies the driver. The ram takes out five hundred CFA francs from his woolen purse, he pays and climbs onto the front seat. The dog takes a thousand CFA francs out of his fur wallet, he pays and climbs into the back seat, with a little shimmy of his backside. The little bird searches in his feather purse, but asks to pay on arrival. The driver lets him to go up on the roof. The truck starts up. A day later, they arrive at the border. The ram thanks the driver, gets out of the truck and leaves quietly. The bird flies away without paying anything. The dog gets out of the back seat and asks the driver for his change. The driver responds:

'Ask the bird!'

This is why nowadays, when a truck arrives, the birds run away, the dog chases the birds but the rams do not move, because only they have paid the price."

Even today, I do not fully understand the meaning of all these stories, but they hold for me the substance of a deep poetry that has an inexhaustible quality. I know they are there, in reserve, available for my whole existence. The legend grows and flourishes like the hibiscus in the garden, which sends us a sign of flowering benevolence in all seasons: it rises in the night of childhood like a comet then, to those who can remember it as the years pass, falls back down again in flakes of light to illuminate our way at each stage of our journey. Before dying, above the river where the beasts go to drink one last time, before the big sleep finally falls over us, it will guide us again, step by step, throwing light on us from afar so that we do not fall.

*

It was Saleh who took me into the hut for the first time.

The hut is deep, it attracts me like a cave. I take a look inside it as soon as I can, as soon as the caretaker is not there, when he leaves to do his round in his big djellaba, his sleeves rustling faintly, his keys clinking. From the inside, I hear the crackling of the radio and the laughter of the women. I have a terrible desire to enter, but the return of the caretaker or a woman coming out of the hut make me turn and flee as if I had the devil at my back.

Saleh noticed my little ploy. One morning when I am playing with the dog in a corner of the yard, he calls me and takes me by the hand. His palms are callused, rough like a millstone. And together, he preceding me as he bows his head gently, we enter into the hut.

My heart is pounding and I'm petrified with fear. But very quickly, on my skin, there is a divine feeling of coolness. My bare feet land on the clay floor, which is so cool and so soft that it seems to make no sound under my footsteps. On this downy earth, my heart rate slows down. Cautiously, as my eyes get used to the darkness, I reach out to the side and feel the walls. The sides of the hut are not rectilinear, or drawn in a straight line: I brush my palm against a series of blocks that have an irregular outline, but are very soft to the touch.

I have a little more confidence now. Saleh has let go of my hand and he is looking at me with a slight smile. I go forward. The soles of my feet touch a sort of checkerboard. A little farther, the floor of the hut is paved with river pebbles. The caretaker sleeps on a slightly raised stone slab (to protect himself from scorpions and snakes, Saleh explains to me later). In another part of the hut, reserved for the women, there are two western-style beds: on the sandy floor, the women have drawn a series of very beautiful circles and arabesques. Stems and petals sketch here and there the shapes of pictograms, flowers, and letters, like a vast alphabet made of black sand.

One thing surprises me: there is no bedroom in the hut. Only three rooms, rectangular in shape, three bare rooms, separated by partitions that do not even go up to the ceiling. I am in the central room and I make out the one in the back, over there in the shadows. I then understand that, as in Scrabble, the rooms can be arranged in several different ways, which are complementary and constantly renewable.

The hut is nothing like a shabby shack or a primitive shanty. It's not a rough cabin or an unkempt hut like I've seen before and will see again in picture books or comics. Of course, the contrast strikes me between my parents' house, which is bright and solid, built as a permanent structure on poured concrete foundations, where all the rooms are covered with white tiling, and the caretaker's hut, with its roof made of straw and metal sheets and its clay floor. In our house, everything is fluid, smooth, we move from one room to another with ease. In the hut, everything is rounded and changeable, shadowy, earthy: even the dust is not an enemy but a domesticated element of the dwelling and the walls, like the spiders' webs or the crackling of the insects that make their nests there. Sounds are not the same there either: sparklingly clear in the house, they are muffled and stifled in the hut.

It is a revelation. Until now, I had thought the hut was a non-house or an almost-house. But I discover that it is simply another way of living in the world and that it protects very effectively from the heat, destitution, and noise.

4

Next to the house, in a corner of the yard hidden from view by a slight slope in the ground which plunged it into half-light even at midday, there was a tree whose foliage was literally made up of the most varied animals, living among the branches in an incredible chaos, battling against each other in memorable jousts and yet coexisting in a paradoxical harmony. It looked like a new species of tree, giving birth to all kinds of animals, offering them shelter and crackling with joy. It was nicknamed the tree of creatures.

In its roots were nesting tortoises, intelligent and placid, but also a few ratels, a sort of short-haired badger, nasty little things with white canines and razor-sharp claws, which launched themselves at the testicles of passers-by. Its trunk sheltered an ant colony, or rather a whole profusion of ants: large black ants, small yellow ants, tiny red ants, no broader than a grain of rice, which stung violently and gave off an acidic smell. Its foliage was full of snakes, which hissed and slipped over it like ropes. Its branches were covered with lizards, crows, and toads, and its top was perpetually capped with some frilled-neck bird or crowned eagle, with its white breast and dark plumage. Everything that runs, flies, jumps, and crawls seemed to have found refuge in this prodigious tree. Buzzards flew above it as swift as the wind.

This is where I learned to speak to the animals and the land, and these exchanges have never left me.

*

Saleh often takes me to the tree of creatures to teach me how to catch them and to learn their secrets. First of all, knowing how to spot an animal's hiding place, guessing its age and its species (rat, snake, mongoose, rabbit …) just by the amount of soil it throws out while digging its hole. Differentiate the hole dug to hide in from the one dug for food (the anteater for example), the one dug to rest. The one made to give birth.

Then we get the traps ready, we prepare the baits. Peanuts for squirrels (they adore them), which will soon be caught in the snares, seeds and a funnel for rodents, and, for birds, a small basin molded into the ground, coated with clay and filled with water, surrounded by slipknots, or simply branches coated with latex acting as birdlime ... Saleh knows a thousand subterfuges, but forbids me to use jaw traps, which make the animals suffer and cripple them. The goal is not to kill, but to capture *alive* and observe: how they move, how they wiggle, wriggle, how they manage to escape us.

This does not mean that at the beginning, on my part, there was not a certain level of ferocity: feed, imprison, pamper, neglect, make them suffer a little, sometimes for nothing, just for the pleasure of possessing or rejecting ... and finally being very attentive, taking lessons from the animal and finding a harmony between its vivacity and our own: it was with animals that I first experienced love, cruelty, and freedom. When you have captured a lark, after hours and hours of watching, all of life is held in your fist. You learn to respect it.

Before humans, teachers, educators, professors, even before parents or family, it was animals that educated me. A rugged fraternity has united us since childhood, an immense complicity mixed with a certain rivalry, as in those stories where the lions come to the village once evening falls to leave meat for the humans, even though they can hunt them mercilessly during the day. Up to the age of ten, I hardly remember my schoolteachers or my first classmates: on the other hand, I have very precise memories of the contours of certain shells, the outline of wings, and the shape of claws.

All these animals arouse in me a touch of apprehension and a violent admiration. They train me to see, to sense things, they tell me when to be wary and when to run away, they teach me to dance and to run. They are the keepers of a certain rhythm, of a pulsation, repetitive and yet infinitely varied, a musical percussion that beats inside my own chest. Above all, without my even being aware of it, they already mark my whole existence with an immense sensitivity to nature, not only in the deployment of its landscapes or the contemplation of its phenomena, but in what one could call the *incandescence of sensation*, which is so alive during childhood, and which we rarely find, later, except in artistic experience or when in love.

The tree of creatures was my first guide and a powerful tutor. I consult it still today, from memory, for every decision that is a bit difficult to make. It reminds me of the essential rules, the infinitely varied laws of the universal, the primordial resources, and the fundamental principles. Where something comes from (bursting the surface of a leaf or piercing the heart of the bark), how things move along, rolling, unrolling (the jolting movements of the centipede, the undulation of the caterpillar), means of attack and defense (the bats that strike the face, ants that bite at the heel). How things finally die, their fangs clenched, their mouths foaming. Thanks to the tree, whatever the disaster, there exists a whole varied, perverse, and polymorphic multitude which ingests and digests, which thrives and poisons, that mates and devours, that runs to my rescue ….

*

Honor to whom honor is due: the dogs. The ones you find in Chad often have scabies, fleas, and ticks: they are earthy dogs, their ears eaten by flies, some thin like green beans, others fat like sausages. But they provide us with some great examples of running and dancing, and our first lessons in anatomy. There are a dozen in and around the yard, and even more cats, rabbits and sheep, chickens, goats, roosters, not to mention our guenon. We sleep with them, play with them, live with them.

Among them, two dogs stand out: one named Dick and the other Sao. The first is of European origin: he was abandoned by his master, a Briton named Richard, who returned to his native island. He has been wandering ever since from yard to yard. His coat is completely black, a beautiful burnt black, almost blue, and is adorned with a red spot in the middle of his forehead. The second is a local dog, a yellow-haired *laobé* streaked with fiery stripes of color. He emerged one day from who knows where, semi-wild but so mischievous and so endearing that he was immediately taken in by my father. Dick often accompanies the caretaker on his rounds.

He is a tall, leggy, and vigorous hound, he scares everyone. Sao most often dozes on the terrace: he is small and very clever, women and children love him, he passes from hand to hand. It is said that he is in contact with the spirits and the ancestors who roam around. Dick and Sao look at each other literally all day, glaring at one another—*Arbout soulbak*: "Get ready!" they seem to say to each other, barking from afar. In the evening, they fight nonstop, in outbreaks of frenzied violence where each one alternately gets the better of the other. By observing them, I learn about both patience and rage.

"Toumaï! Live like a dog!" Amaboua shouts to me. She is the caretaker's eldest daughter, a young woman so charming that it is said that she can stop a whole herd of zebus by the grace of her smile alone. She always calls me "Toumaï," I don't know why. But it's a Chadian name and I like it: thanks to her, I feel like a native child.

"Animals have so much to teach us, Toumaï," she says to me on the threshold of the hut, stroking my hair. "Dogs move from one state to another so easily—they are peace itself, and then rise up like hurricanes. They know no phase of awakening, or transition.

These are for humans only, and they take forever. For dogs, it is the present, all the time. Dogs are palpitations. Toumaï, live like a dog!"

Amaboua is right. This delicate little goat with its tawny and white coat, this lamb chewing its grass, its muzzle fresh, its eyes closed, or even this cat that rears up, its hair bristling: I quickly realize that they have a thousand things to say to me, at almost every moment of the day. This is what we could call the regency of the animals, their different government, their immense unseen knowledge. Animals carry with them an innumerable delegation of secret skills, of hidden know-how, of surreptitious savvy, a whole hidden and yet transparent erudition, to which we must listen if we want to become a man worthy of the name. Toumaï, live like a dog!

*

But even more than the dog or the lion, my favorite animal at the time was the ratel. The ratel is a small badger, all sinew and muscle, with sharp incisors and claws, and appalling aggressiveness. I like his little marten mouth and his two-tone coat: his belly and lower limbs are completely black but he proudly sports a broad white patch all the way down his back that runs from the top of his skull to the tip of his tail. He is in fact, so to speak, the punk rocker of the mammals. He's a Sid Vicious or a Johnny Ramone reincarnated as a carnivore. In those years, the radio stations broadcast to Africa the escapades of this new musical genre, punk, which completely renewed the musical landscape: I gladly associate it with this raging and hyped-up creature.

The ratel is a real tough guy. He never steps back. His skin is so thick that he is not afraid of assegai or spears, so says Saleh, who fears them like the plague and never approaches them. In the bush, it takes at least six lions to overcome them, with considerable collateral damage (bleeding ears, lacerated sides, eyes torn out). In town, there has to be a good number of you beating him like crazy for hours for him to finally succumb. When men attack him, the ratel targets the testicles or the Achilles tendon. He's a fierce trickster and, literally, a cut-throat.

His strategy is to attack. He attacks all the time. He is no bigger than a knuckle of ham, he has a weird look—the unlikely elegance of a cross between the hyena and the koala—but he will attack until the end, until you leave him in peace or until death ensues. He is one of the only animals in the world that can attack while retreating. He's a warrior, he's a boxer, he's always looking for a fight. He walks blithely across tiger territory, prances in the midst of leopards, walks right up to the muzzles and mustaches of lions. He pays no heed to the natural hierarchies, nor to the segregations that are attached to them: he crosses the barriers separating the species and different spaces with a few bites. He is the embodiment of aggression.

In praise of the ratel: to me, still only a child, he shows that even the little ones can be respected. He always arrives with back arched and leaves with his head held high, after handing out a beating to a scorpion or a cobra. He is truly one of a kind. I will learn moreover, many years later, that he is the only survivor of his species (*Mellivora capensis*) in the living world.

Like any highway bandit, the ratel feeds on anything and everything. But he loves wild onions and especially honey. This gallows bird has sweet and sugary tastes: he is the persecutor of bees, the executioner of swarms and hives, the terror of beekeepers. When he swallows a snake, the dose of venom he receives sometimes manages to lay him low for a few hours ... then he gets back up, his stomach full, the venom metabolized, and he leaves as if it were no big deal. Except when it cannot be avoided, death itself wants nothing to do with him.

*

Finding food. Protecting oneself from predators. Raising children. Surviving and helping each other. Watching over your territory. Solving problems related to their environment. It is clear to me, to my child's mind, that animals are like us and that we may even have been created in their image. It seems to me indisputable that some of them are living beings like any others, ambiguous, tortured, and fascinating. They have an inner life (you only have to hear Sao growling or whining in his sleep or see Dick gazing into the distance, lost in thought) and an immense capacity for communicating meaning.

I can see that there are several kinds of young goats: the smart ones, the lazy ones, the fighters, the stubborn ones. I note that Babou the guenon shows her teeth when she laughs, like us, and also when she is afraid, like us. I observe the muscles in their faces, so similar to ours, or the way they wiggle their ears to make us understand something we don't want to hear. For me, it is obvious that animals have a sense of humor: the little goat who insists on pulling my trousers down when we are fighting together in the dust of the yard, without ever hurting me with the slightest scratch, is the most striking proof of this. But they also have a sense of mourning: when the cat Minouche loses one of her newborns, carried away one morning by an Ovampo sparrowhawk, all the cats and dogs in the yard gather in a circle and look at her with a frightened air, not because they say to themselves, like certain humans, that they will no longer see a loved person but, much more profoundly in my opinion, because they have understood that something has just been interrupted in the great vibration of the world.

But the adults, always the adults, with their clear knowledge and their assured tone, tell me that no, it is not possible. The neighbor, M. Delmotte—whose wife herself looks like a little red-haired rodent, friendly and crazed—said to me one day in a learned voice: "You understand, they lack speech!" But I found that they talked, the dogs, the cats, the little goats, the ratels, that you just had to know how to hear them, to listen when they spoke, the snout suddenly upright and the eye sparkling. But no, the humans would have none of it, and just kept repeating: "Animals, they lack speech!" And we, I thought, quite to the contrary, we just needed to know how to keep silent so that, like them, we could raise our heads into the passing winds.

THE OUTDOOR SCHOOL

5

Now the game comes to life and the grid opens up. The letters slide across the racks, consonants are exchanged and vowels swapped, the scores add up. We are seated in the leafy green silence of the yard. The sun dissolves the characteristics and the limits of each object, giving them a slight undulation like overheated corrugated iron. The game board is neat and well set-out, like a map or a diagram, in the center of the table. All around, a red dust rises up, coloring in the landscape, sketching drafts of fences, tentative outlines of branches.

I look up. A drop of water falls from a tap that is not fully closed. Farther away, the noise of trucks fades in the dust of the roads. A palm leaf slips under a wheel, injured dogs run on three legs, we hear them groan or moan, and always this regular, nagging note of water dripping on the yellow sand as it cuts across the yard and penetrates into the surrounding sky. Who then would let a crystal bead drop like that onto a silver tray every ten seconds? For some, it is a bird that did it. For others, a lizard.

I focus on this noise. Various vibrations are emitted, which are like the musical sounds of the voice: to create and adapt words, it takes enormous mental tension. I gather together all these places where the air is so hot on the skin and I write them in blue ink onto the sheet of paper. Then, the possibilities expand, the colors thrive, and the words unfold in all directions.

I look up. I open the gate. I leave the kingdom of the courtyard.

*

It was not enough to know how to read the clouds racing in the sky above or the flight of the birds over the river — you also had to go to school.

I don't remember much about my first school. I was too busy playing with birds and lizards. At the end of primary school, you have to join the big school, the *collège*, as they say. I take the entrance exam in sixth grade, and am admitted. At that time, I am ten years old. Or rather: I am in the second septenary. It was Saleh who taught me to count like that. Saleh had an explanation for everything that happens on Earth. I can still see him fanning the embers under the *kanoun*. Beneath the low ceramic stove, his hand shakes, mixes, stirs—and he pulls from it advice for my whole life:

"Toumaï, human life is subdivided into nine degrees," he says. "And then these nine degrees are further subdivided into three stages, and each stage has three degrees. Each degree corresponds to seven years. So, from birth to our seventh year, we are in the first degree of the lower degree: the child is in his mother's school. He obeys only his mother, he believes only in his mother. Whatever he is told, he will ask his mother, 'Papa told me this, is it true?' Or: 'I saw that, is it true?' He sees things only via his mother for seven years."

"Yes, but I'm ten years old now. I go to the school for the older kids."

"You are in the second septenary, Toumaï. You have passed on to *the outdoor school*." (He puts a lot of stress on his words, as he arranges the coals and embers, which crackle and crack and throw out sparks.)

"I no longer have the right to have fun then?"

"Whether it is an initiation, whether it is with a master or your comrades, it is always school, because everything is school. Going to have fun is going to school. Going to get water is like going to school. Everything is about teaching and learning. Nothing is just recreational. You understand?"

"Yes, Saleh. And after that?"

"From the age of fourteen, that is to say, having passed the second septenary, the child begins to be his own person, separating from his mother, because he is moving towards his twenty-first year. He starts to say to his mother, 'No, you don't understand, it's not like that!' He begins to argue. You will start soon."

"Yes, Saleh. And after that?"

"At twenty-one, you will have finished the little cycle. You are supposed to have made a first round of all the initiations. You will have been told about the immobile living beings. You will

Scrabble

have been told about the mobile living things. In short, you will have been told about the animal kingdom, the plant kingdom, the mineral kingdom. You will deepen this knowledge further for twenty-one years, which represents three more ages. It is only in the fifth septenary, at the age of forty-two, that you will have the right to speak. At that point, you will be a man."

"Yes, Saleh. And after that?"

"You will still have twenty-one years to teach, it's compulsory. You will have to give back what, over twenty-one years, you learned in your youth and developed in your adulthood. You will then reach old age, at sixty-three. From the age of sixty-three, among the Fulani, we say: 'He is out of the park.' You will be a sort of retired person: no one will be able to demand anything from you anymore, you can enjoy your life, but you will be able to give of yourself if you feel like it. By that point, I will be long gone—but you will not forget, will you, Toumaï?"

"No, Saleh. I will not forget."

I have not forgotten.

So spoke Saleh, in cycles and kingdoms and septenaries. Listening to him, I had understood that I would have the right to speak in the fifth cycle of seven years, from the age of forty-two—a period in time that I could not even imagine.

"Forty-two years" appeared to me then as far away as the horizon or the moon in the sky. Today, having passed the septenaries and approaching the moment when I must give back what I have learned, I often think of Saleh's words and it seems to me that the more time passes, the more I understand them.

*

My life as a child at this time revolves around a few simple sayings that are nonetheless always true in their great candor, and that are remarkably precise beneath their apparent naivety:

The fox is smaller than the dog but bigger than the cat,
The panther is a long-limbed cat and much more dangerous,
The hippopotamus is as big as an elephant but he lives in the water,
The giraffe is the tallest of the animals,
The pangolin is bigger than the tortoise but has the head of a monitor

lizard,
The doe is the size of a goat but runs much faster,
The otter has the coat of a dog and the whiskers of a lion ...

By dint of always beginning my thinking with questions of size, scale, and territory, I acquire a mode of reasoning founded on observation and comparison that still serves me well today. The sobriety of these sayings is not without a certain elegance or poetry. It is this alliance—observation, comparison, rhythm—which comes to me from my Chadian childhood and which I try to put into practice.

If everything is school, as Saleh says, I really don't see why I should go to this strange place so far from home that we call "collège." This *collège* reminds me of the glue with which I coat the twigs of acacia to trap birds. I'm afraid of being bored, indeed of getting stuck there.

Fortunately, Amaboua accompanies me: she is already in her third septenary and takes me to *collège* every morning. She smells good. It's nice to walk the streets with her and, without me being able to explain why, it gives me a kind of pride. This feeling spreads right through me when she takes my little hand in hers, which is large and soft, with her long slender fingers around which sometimes, on holidays, henna tattoos wind like snakes.

*

As soon as you are outside, the light changes. It is no longer quite the same as it was in the round courtyard. It is brighter and more varied, it spurts towards the side alleys and changes at each crossroads. In the early morning, the city is calm. The street burns under a little yellow sun. I am going to *collège*.

I lived in a well-ordered little world. A world made up of a living room, a corridor, a bedroom, another corridor to the bathroom and the toilet, a door that opened onto my parents' bedroom. My companions were the furniture, the inexpensive sofa with its somewhat shabby cushions, the chairs that had arms and those that did not. In the yard were dogs, cats, reptiles, and birds. And then there was the terrace, on which I spent the evenings watching the sun go down in the distance into the gold of the river. Now, I am moving out of this circle and I have to learn the new words: suddenly, I hear them in a different way, the word *chaussée*—so flat—and the word *caniveau*—so deep. I rediscover the word *mosquée*, with its acute accent like a small, pointed minaret. I understand that one can pay in cowries or in CFA francs: cowries are shells, which are used as jewelry and as currency. But you can't hang CFA francs on your ears, said Amaboua, laughing. And each one of these words reveals to me whole swathes of reality that I had not known about.

The *collège* is a little far from the house, but I prefer to go there on foot, because the road that leads there opens up a new world, singularly colorful and pulsating with a thousand possibilities: the palm tree topping the hospital with its beautiful green tuft, the gas station with its pumps and pipes that stretch like grass snakes, fallow areas where children my age play ball among cows cheerfully chewing, rubbing their horns against tufts of bulrushes, and trampling the grass under their hooves. So, is that what going to *collège* is? This world, which was only a vague possibility, arranged in pale touches around the yard and of which I only saw fleeting fragments or distant reflections through the fences, suddenly becomes a massive reality, takes on an overwhelming scale and form.

So, every morning, I see very clearly the day coming in, with its clamor and its characters, its sweat and its hopes. I learn, I enter the real life of the country. Children in Chad always carry something heavier than themselves. They are little bundles of power, mobile and hardy. From dawn, they are loaded with a thousand miserable treasures (dates, mangoes, coils of rope, and pieces of leather, which they will sell at the market as soon as class is over)—and yet they seem tireless. Since that time, I have had immense respect for people who carry something on their back: this very burden gives them at once weight and dignity, a sense of gravity. The sun is a hammer that strikes relentlessly and yet, in this flat heat, everyone remains upright in the sky in their own way: women back arched and proud, men sticking out their chests, old people bowed and bent. The way they hold their heads, the strength of their hips, the suppleness of their spines, the power of their necks, and the movement of their pupils, throwing attentive sidelong glances looking for the slightest obstacle—this, still today, is everything that appeals to me in a human being: a certain camber of being, a *bearing*.

My satchel on my back, I hurtle down the dirt, mud, and stone paths. I count the electric poles: there are fourteen planted on my route, I touch them with my hand. They are rough and ready wooden poles but I like to think of them as supports for the race I run: I throw myself at them at full speed and spiral around them, flying off and landing a little farther along. Sometimes I fall to the ground and skin myself to the point of bleeding, but I get up even more joyful from these scratches, like a plant that grows back after a bush fire. My skin takes on all the little colors of creeping roots and climbing grasses.

My nose in the air, I inhale the smells that surround me: the dry, burnt smell of the bush, the cold, wet smell of the forest. The immense, clear scent of the morning, with its little taste of coolness. I quiver, without reason, attentive to the extraordinary things happening in me and around me: a powerful joy takes hold of my whole being and lifts it up into the morning. It is my outdoor school, that of bends and corners, twigs and scrublands, bifurcations. It takes patience. It takes nerves of steel, a certain form of violence, and a taste for experimentation. But if you accept it, it will develop in you a keen sense of observation, a formidable intuition, and, at your risk and peril, an incomparable pleasure: that which comes from taking in the world around you.

6

The Félix-Éboué high school is located in the south of the city. You have to walk for a little while along the Chari, a sumptuous river that the mud and the sun transform into an alloy of silt and silver, then leave the Évolués district on your right to head towards the Chagoua bridge. At that time, the large ivory-white building, pierced with hundreds of small square skylights which let in the light and give it the appearance of a box of dominoes, also welcomed younger classes, those from the *collège*. It is a mixed school, a blend of ages and social conditions, of colors. In my class, there is a bit of everything: blacks, whites, small ones, big ones, kids who have entered adolescence and others who have not left childhood, fully developed young women, with superb busts and arched backs, and others who resemble fragile dolls of ebony or porcelain. Some heads are frizzier than a thorn bush, others are bright blond like the bill of the oxpecker. Dark, smooth skin like cumin oil sits next to pale, powdery skin like tapioca flour. Yet, in the class photo, all the white children are in the first two rows, while almost all the black children are in the back.

I get along particularly well with the shepherd children: they have a smell that I really like, a smell of smoking wood fire in the morning. They arrive from pastures or palm groves, their crooks in their hands, a blue net slipped over their shoulders like a Roman toga, tie their goats and kids in a corner of the school, and go to class. In the afternoon, they leave class to graze their animals or sell them at the market. This great freedom impresses me. At the age of thirteen or fourteen, they are already capable of walking fifteen kilometers alone, finding the right places for grazing, and negotiating the price of a cow. It is even said that some have already slaughtered a ram.

I make friends with Abdelkader very quickly. Abdel, as he's called. Tall, slender, he has a reddish tinted skin and blue-brown

Lycée Annexe N'Djamena 1978-79

eyes as the Tuaregs sometimes have; he's gifted with phenomenal visual acuity. He's nicknamed the Eagle: he sees details with the naked eye that even with my father's binoculars I can hardly pick out. He can spot a little gray sparrow a hundred yards away in the shade of some foliage or a sand-colored snake under the cob of a hut.

A little later, I will make friends with Youssouf, a young Toubou with a bird's nest mop of hair who spends his time whistling melodies (sometimes sweet, sometimes sad) and drawing in the sand with his shepherd's stick. Youssouf is extraordinarily agile: he excels in physical education classes and literally flies from place to place in the playground. We call him fleet-footed Youssouf. Every time I saw him he had his stick in his hand or not far from him: when he comes into class, he puts it in a corner and never loses sight of it. Youssouf and Abdel are used to pulling down the leafy branches to make them more accessible to the little goats, and hold their pens in a very particular way, with great delicacy, their elbows raised towards the sky and the tip bent gracefully over the paper, as if they had at their fingertips a reed stem hanging over a sheet of silk.

Saleh was right: everything is school. Abdelkader and Youssouf teach me practical knowledge: during recess, they explain to me how to prepare animal fodder, choose young branches, grind leaves, and prepare crushed pods, kneading them with curdled milk. They are precious friends. They know which lands are the saltiest (which the livestock prefer), but also which trees provide the best shade (the most sought after by shepherds). They show me how to choose the best dates—light in color, slightly shiny, with a taste of melting honey—and we feast together on seeds from the goldenrain tree and peanut nougat.

At first, Youssouf scares me a little, because his face is completely scarified. The incisions on his face, long and deep, perfectly healed, give him a disconcerting appearance, as if he had cords carved in relief up to the top of his skull. For a child, everything is *monumental*, and even more so that which affects the face. But very soon I will get used to it and he will even invite me to touch them. I can still feel the sensation of that bark-like skin beneath my fingers—ebony braids, cords, stripes—surprisingly soft and rough at the same time.

Later, Youssouf will teach me how to braid grasses to make a whistle. The whistles encourage the animals to drink: as soon as they hear the shepherd's breath pass between the grass strands, they stretch their beautiful brown necks towards the spring and drink in long gulps, with complete confidence. We can then pet them gently. Abdel will also show me the difference between the antelope flute and the gazelle flute: cut from different horns, they do not make the same sound, the antelope is more robust and deeper (the subdued accent of a trumpet), willowy and light for the gazelle (the melody of a lyre).

In the class, there is also Christelle, a big fiery redhead, and Valérie, a reserved little brunette. They are both daughters of soldiers but one could not imagine two girls more different. I'm a little in love with Christelle but I also have a soft spot for Valérie. When Amaboua comes to get me, she sorts everyone out: "Toumaï! You coming?" As soon as I hear her voice, I leave everything and follow her.

In class, everyone in this beautiful little world mixes and coexists without any particular problem. In the playground, there are endless fights. New words flutter around me: Sara, Toubou, Gorane, Kanembu .... There are often little brawls, which flare up as quickly as they die out, unintended quarrels most often settled by a fraternal confrontation. I remember little Dangara: her father is a taxi driver and her mother sells *bili-bili* (a millet beer). And I

remember big Justin: his father is a civil servant at the town hall and his mother a stay-at-home mom. Dangara is smaller than Justin but, as a Chadian proverb says, "You should never look for trouble with short people, because they pick up stones more easily" …. Standing in the middle of the yard, they face each other in silence. He holds his pebble in his left hand, his chest jutted forward. She, standing right in front of him, her left arm raised, the stone by her right thigh, ready to pounce. The battle never happens, it ends with a well-chosen curse and a great burst of laughter. They throw their stones in the dust. But big Justin did not stare Dangara down, and I find this conclusion very pleasing. Dangara smiles. Her smell troubles me. She seems stronger than a lion.

*

The knowledge given to me in class is much more classical than what I pick up in the playground but, to my great surprise, is not as dull as I feared. Above all, I become aware of one essential thing: I understand that understanding gives a very great pleasure.

The subjects are varied and everything interests me: music, mathematics, French, drawing …. Very committed in French-Latin translation, not too bothered about geography, I feast on Greek translations and study history like it is a religion. Only biology seems a little absurd to me: why waste time dissecting a green frog while it's still alive to see its organs continue to beat under its skin, cut and pulled by pins to the four corners of the table, when we can do the same experiment by watching the buffalo toads swarming near the ponds or by observing the eggs of the female agama, white and round like marbles under her beautiful translucent body? On the other hand, I am delighted to be able to put a name to the multiplicity of bones that vibrate under my skin: femur, tibia, ulna, radius, fibula, humerus …

In mathematics, it's more complicated. The teacher, Mrs. B., wears small rimmed glasses that give her a surly look, and has a bun that looks like it was hastily tied at the nape of her neck with frantic gestures, as if she wanted every morning to get rid of her hair by bundling it in the most careless way possible and hiding it behind her head. Youssouf and Abdel hate her. It must be said that she always arrives in class like a fury, calls the register at full speed, then hits us, in her shrill voice that sounds like a guinea fowl, with a math problem far removed from their daily concerns:

"A badly closed tap drips a drop of water every two seconds. If fifteen drops make ten milliliters, how much water is wasted in one minute? I will collect your answers in ten minutes."

"But Miss, at my house there is not even running water!"

"Youssouf, an hour of detention."

"At my house, we go to get water from the well, Miss ...."

"Abdel, an hour of detention."

Laughter bursts out and Mrs. B. remains adamant, bombarding us every time with a new problem to do with pulleys or plumbing. To take revenge for the accumulated hours of detention, Abdel and Youssouf hide a large flying termite with a fork-shaped head in the registration book. When Mrs. B. opens it, there is a general panic: she utters a cry more piercing than Archimedes coming out of his bath and flees, the bun collapsing over her shoulders, like the illustrious scientist running naked through Syracuse, to the cheers and jibes of the students. "The living insect has prevailed over cold mathematics!" Youssouf triumphantly calls out, his fist raised, before being given two additional hours of detention.

Youssouf and Abdel are very good students, but they do not miss a chance to make fun of a form of knowledge that sometimes seems too abstract to them. For them, an airplane is a "Flying Device Imitating a Natural Bird." A boat, an "Aquatic Construction Transporting Natives and Men in Uniforms on Water." Their verve is incendiary and their *joie de vivre* contagious. When I am with them, I develop the habit—which I have never lost—of always seeing the world on many levels. There is an official space, that of knowledge certified by institutions and accredited by the masters, and then an unofficial space, immense and heterogeneous, composed of a multitude of clandestine forms of knowledge, of lateral methods or singular trajectories that have less formal value but are invigorated by laughter and in which words circulate more freely.

*

I learn quickly. I memorize very well. On the other hand, I speak little. I am no good at speaking, almost mute even: I refuse to answer the questions that I am asked and even after being asked several times, which leaves a deafening silence hovering over the class, I do not open my mouth. The teachers try to make me speak through being gentle, persuasion, and threats: nothing helps. I remain silent. Some teachers then say that I am "autistic" (this is the time of the first systematic psychological experiments with autistic children). They summon my parents and want to have me examined by a doctor, but my mother, pointing out my good results in writing, stubbornly refuses. So, I continue to follow the classes, silently. For a sentence to come out of me, I need to have worked on it internally for a long time. It then bursts forth, like a sort of oracle which no one can really make any sense of. After a while, even the most stubborn teachers give up and leave me to my silence. This is how I manage the miracle of being both an excellent student and a complete dunce.

It is also in *collège*, through the eyes of others, that I learn that I am short-sighted. I already knew it, but confusedly: I become fully aware of it through the mockery that is thrown my way. From a very young age, I have worn big golden glasses which cover half of my face, an enormous contraption that gives me the appearance of a scuba diver and provokes the taunts of my fellow students. They burst out in all languages:

"Blind as a bat!"

"Squinty eyes!"

"*'Amyān*! Hey, four eyes!"

"Toumaï the blind man! You see neither at night nor in the day!"

"*Yalla darr*! Come here! Don't lose your glasses, or you'll fall in a hole!"

From time to time, my glasses are stolen from me and are hidden in a corner of the classroom. I then crawl, groping towards the slightest source of light, literally dazed and all over the place, searching for the precious frames, under the din of mockery, grimaces, sneers. People taunt me, imitate my movements, mimic my manners and my squinting.

Abdel plants his big bright eyes in mine and gives me his advice: "You must learn to use your teeth, Toumaï. Do as the parrot! He climbs along the bars of his cage, to open it using its beak." And, matching words with action, he gives me a knife. It is a small, very sharp throwing knife with a cutting edge, with engravings on the flat of the blade: it is no heavier than a feather and no longer than a pen. From then on, I will always have it with me. I never tire of pulling it out of its leather case, looking at it, sharpening it on a stone, throwing it against the surface of a wall or sticking it into the bark of a trunk. It makes me especially dangerous to tables and chairs, trees and fruit. But from that day, the sarcasm stops and everyone leaves me in perfect peace.

*

History, geography .... What notion of the Earth do I have at that time? What idea of France and history? The countries, the continents, all this is very vague for the child I am.

On the classroom walls, the world is in color; in the textbooks, history is in black and white. And, like Abdel and Youssouf, I do not always manage to grasp the relationship between what I read and what I see around me: Bayard the knight, fearless and beyond reproach .... Charlemagne with his flowing beard .... The vase of Soissons .... Our ancestors the Gauls .... And why not "Our ancestors the cobras" while we are at it? Youssouf and Abdel are in tears of laughter at all these stories of broken dishes and hirsute sovereigns. This strange characteristic of the French of always believing themselves more universal than the others amuses them, and they let rip as soon as the teacher's back is turned:

"Our ancestors the anacondas!" jokes Youssouf.

"Our forefathers the barracudas! ...," Abdel retorts.

"Your grandfather placenta, your grandmother malaria! ...."

A thousand funny facial expressions accompany these explosions of wit. On the other hand, you should have heard them bellow out the motto of France: "Liberty, Equality, Fraternity." They swagger a little, imitate the military salute, but the dream speaks to everyone, and there is no longer any irony in their voices.

Sometimes, after class, while eating dates, they tell me about Toupouri country and Moussey country, they tell me about the Moundang, whose traditional chief is called Gong—a resounding monosyllable which makes us wild with joy. Moundou, Mongo, Moussoro .... We entertain ourselves with talk of the Sahel, Guéra, and Salamat, the borders of Boum Kabir and Chari-Baguirmi, Batha, Biltine, and Mayo-Kebbi. The names of the country are like festive garlands: Ati, Dourbali ... Massakory! A wild energy flows through these leaping phonemes. One day, two lines by José-Maria de Heredia remained written on the classroom blackboard:

Like a flight of falcons out of the charnel house of their birth ...
From Palos de Moguer, rovers and captains ...

Youssouf declaims them at the top of his voice, half serious and grandiloquent, half clowning about: "Tired with the weight of their disdainful woes .... Drunk with a heroic and brutal dream!" Then suddenly, with a determined gesture, he erases the poem and writes in chalk this phrase which fills me with joy and which I still know by heart today:

Some Mousgoum people, and some Massa fish at the Gamsay Bongor pond.

And this is how I learned that the world is plural, in the tangled network of expressions from Chad and the French language. This intertwining endures still and I have adopted the good habit of living plurally.

7

Now, the caretaker and his wives welcome me as one of their own in the hut. I am eleven years old. I pass between the stretched-out legs, I drink Libyan red tea, which I love, I taste millet balls, dipped in a sweet potato sauce, with pepper, salt, and lemon. As soon as I cross the threshold, where drifts the sweet smell of grilled ears of millet, I am careful, as Saleh explained to me, not to step over the grown-ups sitting on the mats. I also know that it is forbidden to walk around a seated person. I never say anything and I listen a lot.

Near the hut, there are often female voices singing. Here, everything revolves around millet. Life hangs on the straight, rigid stem of this cereal, its candle-shaped ears and tiny seeds with their subtle green almond flavor. You put millet in water, it swells and ferments, then spread it out in the sun to dry it. It is crushed to detach the bran, it is made into dough, it is stirred with a stick. Amaboua gives me plenty of raw millet flour, pounded with dry dates and mixed with a little water, a delicious, sweet, and fragrant porridge. Nothing is wasted: the date pulp is given to the goats, who savor their meal as much as I do. Glue is made with millet bran and the hulls.

The millet stalk can also be used as plaster for broken wrists, and the leaf is used to wrap beans and peanut paste. I am amazed by the plural power of this plant, its vigor, the abundance of its properties.

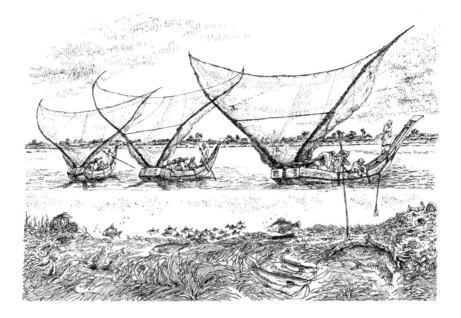

I particularly like the song of the young women who pound millet in rhythm: Amaboua the eldest and Awa the youngest take turns singing. They put all the weight of their shoulders onto the large wooden pestle to grind the millet in the mortar. In front of the hut, their grandfather dozes, barely disturbed—and no doubt even soothed—by the sound of the pestle. The meal is placed on the mat in plates and earthenware dishes. His daughters and granddaughters spread ashes over sorrel leaves to ward off the insects. The sisters are chatting or washing clothes, weaving baskets and hats …. I am eleven years old and I'm starting to notice women.

*

The Chadian women are well-rounded and proud in their bearing, their figures, from the back, from the front, their hair, their overall shape and down to the smallest details. They walk in the town, I meet them on the way to school, the young women in their multicolored clothes: blue, red, gray, or brown, upright and straight like pencils. Whether they are rich and splendid, poor, or sickly, in boubous or in dresses, in cotton or canvas gandouras, or sometimes even in rags, they are beautiful and striking. I like to follow them without knowing where they are going, because they always seem to open up a path through the chaos of the towns, superb silhouettes turned towards the horizon.

Women: they are a rich jewelry store of yellows, greens, reds, a great bay window of phonemes and sounds. Even a child is aware of this. What a joy to walk close by these perfumes and these bodies, these sources of energy.

It often starts with smell, that of their make-up, or of the creams, all these subtleties to which a child cannot give a name, the ointments and the balms that permeate the skin. Awa uses a paste made from sugar and lemon to depilate, which gives her a little citrus scent when she passes, and which goes perfectly with her sharp laughter. Amaboua uses hot mahogany sap, which makes her pull a few funny grimaces, to tattoo herself: her biceps are tender and round, dark, with woody scents and orange undertones. My eyes slip from one girl to the other on the threshold of the hut and I fill my lungs with each movement they make. Each time they move, they let out a bouquet of wild, subtle, or sharp aromas: it is a floral celebration, a fragrant poem.

Tonight, they are going out. Amaboua mixes oils and spices, pats her neck, and, before leaving, spreads a few sesame seeds through her hair. This is *karkar*, the supreme philter. Tonight, everyone will fall under its spell. Watch out for the green pigeons, which eat the fruits of the fig tree .... She sneaks out of the hut and her smell falls on me like a wet towel over my skin. It's a stunning scent. When the gate opens, I hear the sound of jewelry ringing on their ears and their wrists, a party of sound on their twisting silhouettes.

They have a cinnamon apple skin, almond eyes, a vanilla pod for eyebrows and papaya buttocks. They glow at night. "It's like pottery, Toumaï. It's smoothed with oil, pigment, and baobab seeds," Awa explains to me. "You have to glow to be beautiful, it's important."

And then there is their mother, who also makes an impression on me. The caretaker has several wives, but she is the first of them, the oldest. Where does all that beauty go with age? The beauty of her daughters, where did it go to? It is still there, if you look closely, in that way of walking, which is dignified, flexible, and sumptuous at the same time, her head held high perched upon her neck and looking at you like an eagle looks at you from the top of a roof. It is still there, in the line of her shoulders, which undulates while she leans towards the teapot then straightens up with an unexpected suppleness. In her face and in her eyes especially, I can see that her beauty is concentrated there, more intense perhaps than during her younger years, because it is more serious now, as if *enflamed* by the passage of time. The beauty of women does not disappear with age, only a fool would think that: simply, it diffuses, it vaporizes so to speak and disperses to all the aspects of the face, right up to the wrinkles at the corners of the eyelids, which are like wild plants. It is there, in the clear eyes of youth as in the piercing eyes of old age.

Amaboua has tied a green scarf around her head. She is sumptuous, as if she had come out from behind a curtain of leaves. Her nose is long and thin, her mouth has a little twist. She is a canoe on the rapids of the river, a masterpiece of nautical elegance, a schooner of sweetness launched on the waters. She stands at the bow and goes to cast the triangular net. She always looks fragile, you are afraid of breaking her if you brush against her, and yet she gives an impression of power, like a phosphorescence.

Her sister, on the contrary, is fire. I see her very full body, Awa, waiting for her sister at the gate, half outside, half inside. I am beginning to know her tricks. She is a constantly changing snake who uses her curves as weapons of combat, drawing them and sheathing them again, her buttocks swaying and her breasts rocking, setting fire to the surroundings. I see the toe of her left foot digging into the ground, tracing circles and triangles in the red earth, all her insolence in this left foot. She stands upright and gleaming, and throws her sparks at all the boys passing by, who twist their necks to catch a better sight of her, but never take hold of her. She has her own way of standing firm and shying away at the same time, sometimes hugging one of them by the neck, wrapping her arms round him like a propeller before pirouetting and leaving to spark off somewhere else. If she catches a young man, she promises him an eternal love, like faith sworn over the entrails of a sheep—and then she leaves with a great burst of laughter as she turns her back on him. Quite the opposite of her sister, Amaboua, who is lighter, more detached, and tougher than a green banana. I think about them all the time, from morning right through to evening when I do my homework, and I have only one thought, to go out and look for them.

There are also these gestures and these utterances that we do not understand but that set you thinking, these words and these glances whose meanings are obscure, that we pretend to have grasped but which we ponder for a long time once evening comes, because we don't really know their real meaning. Saleh, for example, who warns me, though I'm not yet old enough to understand this warning: "Women, sometimes they burn like metal, sometimes they melt like caramel ...." The conversations of adults are full of these phrases slyly stated: the child listens to them as if they were nothing, but taking in everything, connecting—and for a long time—sex to the clandestine.

My comrades, who are a little older, seem to know much more than I do about it. So, when Dangara disappears from school one fine morning—we will never see her again:

"She had a 'traffic accident,'" explains Youssouf, ironically. Then, seeing my distraught look: "No, she got pregnant, you know! By Justin, the son of the town hall clerk ...."

In this country where everything is as thin as can be, I wonder how this little young woman was able to get big so quickly. And, most importantly, why would it force her to leave school? Abdel tries to make me understand:

"It must be said that she was gifted for having children, that one: you only had to touch her!"

The girls are not to be outdone. Amaboua asks Awa, who has seen Abakar's "jaguar" (I didn't know he had one), details on its size and shape: "candle-shaped like millet, a bunch like dates, or even feather-shaped like sorghum?" Then they both burst out laughing, looking at me.

And then this one, even more enigmatic, heard while passing before the caretaker's hut: "Ah that one! She doesn't use her buttocks just for sitting down!"

What else does she use them for then?

In the evening, before sleeping, for hours I ponder these mysteries that are beyond me.

Finally, there is this funny ballet, at night, around the huts or on the strip of land by the neighboring crossroads. These women sitting on the sidewalks or wandering around under the lampposts, who stare with an air simultaneously terrible and nonchalant at the cars going by … I spend entire nights at my bedroom window spying on them, while sharpening Abdel's knife on the window frame. They have a way of leaning their body over when a car stops, their hips to the side as if to dance a java, their shoes clicking on the soles of their feet, provocative right to the tip of the heel. From behind, they look like crocodile-cows, with their buttocks like blocks of butter or, for the youngest of them, the dongola mares I have seen jumping on the riverbank, their rump reaching backward and pointing skyward.

The windows are lowered, hands pass through the car door, the notes folded lengthwise and held between their fingers. One of the women comes forward, languid like a vine. Glances, whistles, negotiations … A man offers a ribbon and earrings, another a live chicken that he holds with its head upside down, its corn-yellow legs tied up along his leg. She responds to everyone, glancing to the side, her fist on her hip, like a real Carmen, and I understand the strength of this Mérimée that we have just studied in class, who manages to set the undulating creatures down on paper. Observing this merry-go-round every evening, it seems to me that I am beginning to understand. They are scary because they burn, and because they burn they attract. Sometimes they squat down and the jet of their hot piss smokes on the pavement in the night air, just as their fresh and open laughter rises and becomes entwined with the creepers. There is something sinister about them, but also something fragile and joyful, wonderfully human.

This one chews endlessly on gum, which she spits into the dust when a customer arrives—a small, short burst of saliva that greets the newcomer with great disdain. Then she kneels. She is a carnivorous plant. Under the lamppost, her mouth is an orange-yellow berry, her skin is smooth like that of a melon and her protruding lips are shaped like a pear. The other one is a statue, she never moves, even when a man in a cap gives her a colossal slap on the buttocks, which sounds in the night like a gunshot and makes me close the window as quickly as possible, in a panic, to go and hide in my bed.

It was by observing this nocturnal choreography that I gradually understood. There are the forage-girls, those who work in groups, the lawn-girls who lie down immediately, and the plant-girls who lead customers, taking them by the arm—sometimes even by their genitals—to the cabin nearby. From time to time, even in the dark night, I summon up all my courage, I slip my knife into my pocket, and I go out through the window. I cross the yard, hugging the palisades of straw. I go out through a hole in the fence, behind the banana trees, through which the dogs slip in and out during the day. I head for the cabin behind the lamppost, whose old wooden door has no lock or latch. All around, I come across shadows brushing against each other, grown-ups, a procession of ghosts groping towards the half-open door. I avoid the small round square in front of the cabin, I hug the walls and slide towards the open window at the side. There, I lift myself up on tiptoe: I open my eyes wide through my big round glasses, I look as intently as I can into the room. I hear moans and groans, but I see nothing but darkness, everywhere is black, night outside and night inside.

8

For the little guy that I am, slowly passing from childhood to adolescence, sexuality is an opaque, mysterious domain, hidden in the silences of adults, somewhere between embarrassment, fear, and laughter. I remember very well, for example, the sheep sacrificed by the caretaker in the yard—one of those proud wild sheep who learn here how to keep a lookout, to run, to race: suddenly, his big balls are sitting there, in the dust, definitively immobile. Already, during the sacrifice, while the women boiled the rice and prepared the vegetable stew, I was surprised at the attention paid to this part of the sheep by the men who carved up the beast: the strip of skin starting from the base of the belly and plunging between the legs, that which bears the testicles, was removed at the very end and carefully put aside, like a cursed share or like a choice cut.

The animals, who had always been my teachers in everything, once again direct me in my questions, making me think by the form of their actions alone, by their frenzy as much as by their perseverance. From the top of the terrace or in the schoolyard, with vague concern I watch these dogs suddenly struck by a sort of rage, mating like two organisms simultaneously superpowered and sick. The virulence of their act makes me laugh and alarms me at the same time. With Abdel and Youssouf, laughing together, we approach, we observe their "penis"—a word just taught to us by our biology teacher, whose lessons suddenly seem much more exciting to us. Youssouf calls it the *yuna* and Abdel (who has some knowledge of Classical Arabic) the *zob*. Sometimes, some dogs spend whole afternoons literally stuck together, their genitals flushed red, their eyes bloodshot, and their tongue hanging out. They have red genitals at the back and a red tongue at the front. Abdel is overexcited, he violently whips the ground with his shepherd's stick several times, right in front of the animals that are feverish and exhausted from having mated for so long: "Red!

Red! He has a red cock and a red tongue! As if he had a cock in the ass and it was coming out of his mouth!" That's the way that childhood imaginations work.

Coitus has always made me laugh. The copulation of dogs in the public square, the sex that comes out and is exhausted, purplish then streaked with blue veins, the crooked mouth of the mastiff, its frenzied grunts, the cries of adults to separate them, half-scolding and half-laughing, the big tubs of water or millet beer poured on the animals' backs to unhitch them: I often think that the love stories of humans are hardly more glorious than these moments of drooling and bewilderment, of hasty hookups, then painful separation, finished off with plaintive calls and loud moans. A life lesson.

But there is also this strange and secret link, which suddenly announces itself in the middle of a coming-together, and which is more mysterious, more fascinating, more frightening too. Suddenly, two beings look at each other, are moved, and I feel clearly in the intensity, in the way they look at each other in this moment, that something is happening that no longer has much to do with the muddled agitation of these conjoined dogs, their grotesque panic, their confusion, even if it is sometimes still there in flashes and bursts, the knee jutting out on the ground, the pang of desire, the dread mixed with joy of its fulfillment.

*

I believe that it was with Amaboua that I found out, for the first time, what love is.

She arrives, and it is like the hut has changed shape. Space reforms itself, following the contours of her slender blue figure. She floats, she flies, she rises above. Amaboua is beautiful, with her long braided hair running down her back and making it seem like she hovers everywhere. Her nose is long and her mouth a little crooked: her father says that she is cute like a *kimambilo*, the black bird with the long, slightly curved beak. A soft click, when she lowers her eyelids: her look is like a padlock, once it has taken you, it locks you in, you will never forget it. Her eyes the color of roasted coffee fix you with surprising intensity: I know well the fixity of her round pupils and what it means. She wants something.

Other times, on the contrary, she can throw you a look that makes you melt like a sorbet under its gaze.

Her ankles are light, so light, and when she dances, her steps weave on the ground a network of soft lines which are immediately erased in small swirls of dust. She sings, or rather she hums, her tender voice reveals the words by enveloping them in a multiplicity of whispered breaths in varied notes. Her shoulders and legs are round and curl around this shimmering melody. She murmurs tender words, the meaning of which we cannot guess but whose music we perceive, to some invisible lover whom she holds onto in her dreams. And still her head leans towards a corner of the hut, as if she were looking elsewhere, as if she were thinking of a distant prince.

Her distant prince is Abakar, I know that. I saw their little ploy, everyone saw it, during the preparation of the sheep. I followed them behind the hut, I saw Abakar plunge his face into her black neck, exactly where her guava smell simmers. I heard her laugh loudly then slip away, laughing and leaping as she escaped.

But in the evening, she returned. She knows that I'm watching her. With my big glasses that make me look like a fly, I'm not very discreet, but that doesn't seem to bother her. This time, while everyone is busy sacrificing the sheep, it's she who kisses him near the big jujube tree. And she is the one who takes him to the cabin on the neighboring strip, while in the yard, all around the sheep, the songs begin to rise up. Quickly, I know the way, I go to the open window at the side. I see them, he talks to her, he calls her *seyenda*, my love, my kid, my little chick, she smiles and it's her smile that opens the door. He kisses her furtively on the neck, she bats her eyelashes and it is this fluttering that opens the door for him.

I hoist myself on tiptoe and I see for the first time her bare belly, the violent suppleness of her navel. At that moment, I know that her body is a precious stone. I hear the rustling of her white cotton garment falling onto her feet. My throat is dry and I'm breathing harder and harder. Everything seems to be in suspense now, hanging on the clinking of a bracelet on the bedpost, the light glinting off an earring. I watch their movements, the way they lean towards each other and embrace, this whole journey of sweetness. Finally, she sucks in the air with all her strength and stretches out like a rope, then falls back on the bed of straw, like a flower, in pieces. She stays there for a long time, her chest beating, her head to the side, facing the wall.

A few minutes later, after she gets dressed and comes out of the cabin, she notices I am there by the window:

"Toumaï! What are you doing there?"

She is surprised, a little embarrassed, and looks to the side two or three times, twisting her handkerchief between her fingers. Suddenly, inexplicably, she leans towards me, spreads the hair from my cheek and kisses me fiercely. Her mouth is sweet. My heart is pounding at full speed, like the pestle in the millet mortar. I am eleven years old and I discover the combustible power of kissing. Then she leaves, or rather she flies off, she evaporates on the desert wind, like perfume leaving a bottle.

My head is spinning. Her smell still floats around my cheeks. Alone in the night, I learn a truth, which has never left me: some women are the privileged messengers of the deepest meaning that one can hope to find. They are inordinately beautiful, inaccessible and deep, fickle and assured in their very fragility. And when they are in their flow, free and provocative, they eclipse every force on Earth.

9

Outside, always outside. I delay the moment to go home as long as I can. I love the evening, the slow descent of colors over the earth, the orangey sky and its blue suddenly riper, deeper. I love the cries of the birds and the monkeys that rise up when the sun flees, when the temperature cools, because it is the moment when the former return to the nest and the latter set out to pick leaves, flowers, seeds, and fruits, all swallowed up in the feast of their cries.

My parents don't stop me from going out, but they don't like me coming home late. Like all parents the world over, they forbid me from hanging around outside. The problem is that I disobey. I disobey often. I disobey almost all the time, a habit that will bring me many setbacks later. I am "in-cor-ri-gible," says my mother, who likes this word very much, carefully separating its syllables. And yet, she knows nothing about my nocturnal escapades, especially that the faithful Régis keeps watch, going so far as to place duffel bags under my sheets in a vaguely human form that throws them off track. He complains, but he protects me and, when I get home, never calls me out. As for me, I walk, I already walk a lot, free all day and wandering around with my head in the wind. I go out, at any hour, at night too—a habit I have not lost. I slip away especially when the evening comes, I leave. I wander. I am fish, bird, petal. Or, as Saleh says, the king of "quick getaways."

*

In Scrabble, once the first word is found, the subsequent words are placed parallel or perpendicular to a word already positioned. Likewise, I move around the city in relation to a fixed center, the house, from which I move away in ever-expanding circular movements.

The child reasons by circumstantial complements of place: here, there, over there, farther. From point to point, he embroiders a lace pattern of places. The terrace ... the yard ... the town .... And, in the town, district by district, in successive circles, sometimes going very far from the starting point.

I also like to represent life as a spiral, which with each step takes me towards new places, new discoveries. A vortex.

In my childhood imagination, this gives something like this:
—The bed
—The bedroom
—The house
—The terrace
—The yard
—The river
—The neighborhood
—The city
—The world
—The universe

I don't think by neighborhoods but by traces, I advance in successive waves, by irradiations.

As far back as I can remember, I have never done my homework very seriously. My only desire: to go out. I have no idea what I want to do later and, frankly, I don't really care. Bush doctor, archaeologist, acrobat, football player .... These are the professions that interest me, those that I mention when I am asked. People who move around, dig, explore, juggle, and play .... People whose job is literally to be outside, in the field.

By dint of walking, often barefoot, the soles of my feet are covered in calluses, like those ungulates that scrape the ground with their hooves to try to uncover more salty soil. I sometimes imagine that, like an oryx or an addax, these light-footed, saber-horned antelopes that fly between the dunes to escape the hunters, I leave my fingerprints on the ground all over the city and that an eagle could follow me from the highest clouds. Or even that a paleontologist of the future, looking for prints of animals that have disappeared in the clay of long-buried cities, could also find mine, know the frequency and the route of my trips, and even the number of fingers I have or the width of my fingernails. Curiously, while I was still a child, I imagined myself an endangered species, sketching a fossil script on the page of the city, both to escape the hunt and to leave a tangible mark of my presence, between vestige and vertigo.

Sometimes, a simple clump of trees shaken by the wind and dancing in the distance is enough to divert me from my path. I never tire of walking up to these trees, approaching their trunks until I touch them. I want to undo the mental image of it in order to find again, behind the abstract lines penciled on the background of the sky (a triangle of branches, the curve of foliage, a hibiscus ball cut out on the line of the horizon), the truest possible feeling of their own existence: the weight of the wood, the scent of the petals, the red tenderness of the buds. So, I walk and I walk, and I pursue each plant, each animal, and each flowering shrub, to the point of losing my mind.

Twenty steps to the south and twelve to the east: I discover first the hospital and the morgue, which are the two buildings closest to the house—life had put us there, between the hospital and the morgue. Then, the whole landscape around us: the scrawled musical score of the small white-and-black houses which punctuate the city, the walls pierced with rectangular openings which act as windows and give it the appearance of a set of dominoes, the surrounding alleys where the oxen pull the carts loaded with millet, the black-and-white boulevards which transform into yellow and red tracks as they approach the bridges which cross the river, the savannah which sometimes penetrates right into the villages, when the vegetation becomes scarce, when the fences fray, when the roads change into paths and the paths into trails that wind their way along the edge of the dunes, trampled only by the slow pounding of the camels.

I am a bouncing ball, a wandering dog, I am wild thought. I devour the space, I breathe it in deeply. I walk, I venture farther and farther, I go up to the northern part of the city or to the west, I weave through the alleys, come out upon the wonder of the river with its sparkling eddies and its golden sulfur bubbles, its banks laden with acacias and mimosas from which the children dive in, laughing. Then I do a full turn and disappear along the riverbank. Sounds of water. The path to Chari is sandy and slippery. The flowers of the flamboyant tree garland the road with their dazzling petals (I think of my mother, who loves them so much). I see the banks again, the islands, the pirogues loaded with fish. I bring all of this back to life.

*

Soon I'm no longer content with just watching the spectacle of the city: I want to participate in it. I open doors, I push gates, I enter gardens. I climb steep slopes. The smallest footpath, the smallest ravine, seem to me to stand out of the splendor of the terrain, an opening into which I must venture. I move sideways, step by step, extending my arm, then my hand. In this country where you sleepwalk through the heat, I venture out like a skater on the ice. I go into each alleyway, I pass via dead ends, pilfering in the backyards: fruits, cassava, and cakes, stored under the leaves, between clay and reeds.

Régis quite often accompanies me, as does Youssouf, who is very useful to us with his talent for the whistle. As soon as someone comes by as we are thieving, he emits short and repeated whistles (the stride of a caretaker), prolonged and deep (the step of a matron), or very high (the shout of a trader). Youssouf is the perfect lookout. It must be said that his father is a policeman. I have seen him several times at the roundabout where the statue of Félix Éboué is located. He uses his whistle as a natural appendage, resolving any traffic problem with a series of sound variations ranging from a languid invitation to a furious order— little nonchalant toots, an escalation of sounds, a shrill storm over the hoods of the cars …. Youssouf, as a son worthy of his father, whistles as soon as he is given the opportunity, alone or in a group, melancholic or joyful, studying or idle. He doesn't even need a whistle, because he draws incredible sounds from the thin stream of air flowing between his tongue and his mouth. I like Youssouf: extraordinarily fast, he shows us places where his suppleness allows him to slip in, and between him, constantly warbling, Régis who grumbles all the time, and me who never speaks, we form a funny trio, improvised and musical. We *harmonize* very well. With Abdel, on the other hand, communication becomes more difficult, more distant. He comes to class less and less. One day, I see him pass, but he does not greet me. He is in deep discussion with a band of soldiers.

Scrabble

I am a son of N'Djamena: I like its shape, like a shell tilted to the curve of the river, its smells of shiny leaves and baked clay that rise up with the rain, the sonorous haggling in the theater of its streets. And above all I like its name, that initial impulsion carried by the stunning streaks of the N, the incisor of the apostrophe which gives it a superb vitality, the hissing of the consonants which fuse towards the vibrato of the vowels, the final *a* which opens like a compass rose ... N'Djamena, my city with its vibrant heart.

*

Little by little, I begin to understand the city, I begin to understand life. All these scattered elements, these turns and these detours that I know so well, I can now conceive of them as a whole, bring them together and adjust them like Scrabble tiles or see them arrange themselves relative to each other on the map that hangs on the office wall in my father's barracks.

I see the three parts of the city. First, the circular boulevards and the main avenues to the west, where the embassies and the ministries are concentrated, the central bank, the presidential palace, and the parliament building. Here, we find residential districts with white enclosed villas, where black and white vehicles circulate, always air conditioned, as cold as a fridge door, as polished as a pair of shoes. Avenue Charles-de-Gaulle draws a line towards the south, along it are arranged restaurants and bars, a cinema and nightclubs, the offices of airline companies (Air France, Air Afrique, UTA).

Further east, away from the river, the small traders' district, where officials also live: this one revolves around the large mosque and the market, which spreads into the neighboring streets: here, there are only bright colors and the sound of mopeds, the clamor of barter, and the smell of cloves.

Finally, between the two, the Bololo: the popular neighborhoods of the old "indigenous town." The Bololo is a city within the city. Large tarred quadrangles surround ramshackle, narrow, and noisy streets cluttered with loose rubbish, bags, sheaves, dried straw, dirty linens, water containers lying in the puddles. A terrible neighborhood made of mud and dirt: "Of hippopotamus shit," say the residents of other neighborhoods, who rarely venture into it.

These three parts leave a very different visual impression, immediately perceptible to the eye of a child who finds himself confronted with it all at ground level. Between the three, there are relations of domination and resistance that I can sense, that I cannot explain, but I already guess that they are of incredible strength and complexity.

Our house is located in the southeast, just on the edge of the Bololo. It's a pretty quiet area, whose reputation suffers a little for being so close to the Bololo. When I go north, the district becomes commercial, then urban. The houses with sago palisades give way to two-story villas enclosed by triple gates. When I go down to the south and past my family home, everything that is stone turns to earth, the electricity poles tilt and then suddenly disappear, and you know that you have just left the city.

In Scrabble, I particularly like the possibility of branching off from a word already played to a new meaning which, without completely covering over the preceding one, suddenly offers each player a sort of unknown potential and a *salvo* of supplementary openings:

ER

OVER

COVER

COVERED

DISCOVERED

This shimmering quality of Scrabble, which allows you to go, in a few moves, from a word indicating hesitation to a great discovery (through the whole range of openings and coverings), has always seemed to me a good method for exploring a city: working through the setbacks, creating surprises, looking for the dazzling things.

N'Djamena, my city, my childhood.

Am Djemena, which means "the place where we took rest," is the most exhausting city there is, but it was this place that taught me everything. Flowers climbing up a wall like oleander buds along a white dress, powerful fig trees attached to the base of a rock, the river below that stretches under the trees like a lead-colored snake, an imam who calls to us, shouting, railing like a goat, a mother and her child who pass by hand in hand, a soldier falling asleep, his helmet in the dust, by the side of the road …. It is here, in this herbarium of subtle sensations and dazzling thoughts, that I learned that beauty is a climbing force or a bush that repels, that tranquility is deceptive, that happiness is fleeting, that human beings are complex, that poverty reigns and anger rages, that life is fragile but that it can also flourish in the most unexpected, most unlikely places. Every day, without even realizing it, I capture and collect fragments of this knowledge at work, which will follow me all my life—and, to this day, I feel like the son of this off-center capital, this precarious but proud city, arisen entirely from the solitude of the sands.

10

Now I'm going faster and faster and farther and farther. Maybe that is what it amounts to, after all, *growing up*. The first step was taken with Saleh when I dared to enter the hut, the second with the school, where I was obliged to go, but I feel that I have to push farther, and take the decision myself, alone, to somewhere of which I know nothing and where I am not expected to go. This place is quite simply in front of me, since it is located just opposite the house: the Bololo.

With Youssouf, I constantly weave from one side of the city to the other. Children go everywhere. But when I find myself in front of the Bololo, I dare not enter. Even Youssouf, who is usually so carefree, never enters there. His fleet-footedness does not carry him over to that side. Of course, depending on the neighborhood, everything changes: the streets, the houses, the clothes, the voices …. The very gestures are different, the way people look and walk: laughter for example does not ring in the same way, it is shriller and more sure of itself in the fancy neighborhoods, and more discreet and stiffer near the mosque, higher and more unruly in the vicinity of the bush. I realize that each zone—right up to each section of wall—has its characteristic, its particular profile. But the Bololo is something else altogether.

We are not blind to the poverty of the city, even if at this age we are not aware of its extent and gravity. Even in the fancy neighborhoods, we sometimes come across beggars or disabled people, mutilated by jumping on a mine in the north of the country, where war is raging. But the Bololo is even worse.

Habena, Boutal-Bagara, Atrone, Moursal, Chagoua … at the time of which I speak, these appellations do not exist yet, they are just nameless areas of mud. Masses of peat and grass where children wander around in poverty. Large vacant lots where the huts sink into the land, strewn with planks of wood, basins with holes in them, scrap metal buckets shredded by rust. From time to time, huge eruptions of yellowy liquid or earth, like spontaneous gardens of garbage appear over a few days, carrying heaps of crates or packing plastic, cans or shredded tires, poultry bones, leftover meals. In the middle of this cesspool, there are brown or blackish houses, spongy, decomposing, with walls made from bundles of reeds and mud plaster, topped with withered straw. Here, all the houses are unfinished. Even new, they are in ruins. The cement is still in the bags, iron rods eaten away by rust point to the horizon. When the foundations are in place, the concrete casing remains in the open air, its stomach opened, like a boned chicken carcass.

Below, the earth. Above, sheet metal. Between the earth and the sheet metal are people. I observe them from afar, I see them bobbing their heads as they listen to the radio. The crumbling walls of the huts allow streaks of mud to flow, and you can hear the continual quarrels and guess the sordid goings-on in their overcrowded rooms. In this war-torn country, the infirm and the crippled are legion: they stand at the entrances of the Bololo, a cracked cup at their feet, a bandage over the eye or a dressing on the stump. Most are covered with scabies. This district collects misfortunes like meat attracts flies. They are not only without teeth, but without legs and without arms, without hands and without fingers, people with lice and people with ringworms. Hunger and disease are on the prowl: they roam everywhere in the city, but here, they are at home, they reign in Bololo.

What is behind these walls? This question keeps haunting me. From the terrace opposite, I can easily see the outskirts of the neighborhood. The Bololo attracts me, repels me, and fascinates me in the same movement, irresistibly. One day, I will go into this Bermuda Triangle hidden behind the cob walls covered in twisting vegetation.

*

If I dare not enter the Bololo, there is a place where I am particularly comfortable: the market. Unlike the Bololo, you enter when you want, as you want, you are always welcome there, greeted by lively interjections, gestures or grimaces, smiles. Light, faces, brightness … and, above all, the endless stories that ricochet around every day of the week and begin again on Sunday between the salt and the sugar, the clusters of dates and the bouquets of flowers: I like everything in the market.

Right from the entrance, it's a universe in itself, with its own logic and its crazy diversity, which grabs you and holds you there. The air there is green, a dark and moist green in the covered market, and a fresher and less intense green in the surrounding alleys. You swim in the scent of leaves, onion and peanuts, fertilizer and fuel, confectionery, rice mashed in honey. You are struck by the scarlet splendor of the great quarters of meat, caught in the throat by the terrible stench of the red meat and the tanned leather, the harsh and off-putting smell of fresh hunted game, all the streaks of flesh in its palette of scents (raw, refrigerated, dried), its immense heterogeneity.

Right next to their skinned peers, in an incongruous and cruel proximity, the livestock is on show: woolly sheep and furry sheep, Sahelian Fulani sheep, without forgetting the Barbary sheep, with their striking name and yet their fragile grace. Cattle, goats, sheep, horses, camels, and hanging over it all an enormous buzzing sound, like the single vibrant flight of a matron fly. Here more than elsewhere, the fight against the flies is unending. Among the insects, they form a very particular species, innumerable and buzzing, elusive and omnipotent. All shapes, all colors, all conditions. Small, large, black, red or blue, green, royal or domestic, imperial or workers, they buzz and are everywhere. They fly, walk and swim, live underground, in water and in the air, in the forage of the lofts as on kitchen sink draining boards. The fly, the fly will overcome everything.

Not far from the meat market, next to the millet market, is the fish market: fresh fish, dried fish, smoked fish. Placed flat on large blocks of ice, the bingas, the gargas, the salangas are open, skinned, and deboned, suspended by their fins from strings or wound onto sticks. Smells of smoking, wood or grass, float over the mats. I approach and watch. I like to compare the harp-like slender body of the makalele fish with the funny roundness of the balloon-shaped doup-doup. I lean in even closer, above the blue-green scales. You can find everything in the belly of fish: leaves, seeds, crustaceans, insect larvae, seaweed, and very small mollusks, fragments of corals. A whole tiny interior life teeming, invisible, which nourishes the powerful bodies of carp and captain fish.

I wander between the pallets of fruit, the piles of papayas and oranges, grapefruit and plums, avocados and lemons. I taste the local mangoes, wild, fibrous, without juice, or those that literally explode on the tongue, whose softness invades the mouth, the juice flowing onto the chin. I admire the Roberval scales, their huge cast-iron body and the yellow copper pans warped by time. They have pride of place among the stalls, accompanied by an armada of diamond-shaped weights, which the traders handle at full speed as they chant numbers, passing from the fruit to the pan, from the pan to the hand, from the hand to the fingers and from the fingers to the bills, literally juggling between cast iron and fruit, to arrive at an end result that is always very precise and very random—because in their great wisdom they know: they know that here everything is weighed and nothing is calculated, that they will never manage to quantify everything, to evaluate everything, that this is not even desirable, that it would be absurd to claim to reduce the reign of diversity, that it is not the aim of all this trade, that it would be the end of the market and the start of war, that real trade is an endless phrase than can only really be concluded, temporarily, by an exchange and by a smile.

But above all, I realize very quickly, the market is the realm of women. Beverage sellers, crop carriers, cake deliverers, fishmongers or tea makers, cooks or food sellers: they keep silent, but they are the real bosses of the market. They count, they measure, they regulate everything. Like all of the men, Saleh often makes fun of them, their age or their weight ("Look at that one, if she's on a diet, it's a banana diet!"), but he fears them like the plague and they always get the better of him in haggling. Wisely sitting behind the wobbly wood of the low tables at the edge of the tarmac, or perched on metal stools in front of a stall of fabrics or fresh food, these all-seeing women know everything that goes on in the market. A single word from their mouth, a verbal rocket, can make or break prestige, destroy or create a reputation. Saleh knows this, and I notice he showboats behind their backs but politely buys soap or eggs from them, then runs away without asking for his change. Yet the harsh smile of these women can express in an instant astonishing tenderness: when they see me pass by, they grab me by the shoulder and give me a nice round donut, a croquette of millet, or a cassava cake.

Finally, there is the snack bar, my favorite place, and probably the most frequented. It welcomes everyone, in an aroma of fried potatoes and flour cakes. On the ground, there are loose matches, cigarette butts, pits of fruit chewed and spat out in the dust. In the air there is the giant emblem of a bottle of Gala beer in the three national colors (blue, yellow, red). They serve industrial or artisanal drinks—Fanta, Coca-Cola, local beer, palm wine—and also an excellent *boule rouge* with okra sauce, which lands on the plate in a lively clamor, in a fairyland of colors: pepper green, millet red, and a pinch of yellow pepper.

The market is near the grand mosque, we come across Muslims there, animists, and Christians, which does not prevent intrigues of all kinds. Here, people always seem to move between shenanigans and haggling, chicanery and conspiracy. So much so that we sometimes wonder if the small sachets nailed to the entrance of certain stalls contain a drug or narcotic, spices or an aphrodisiac, or even some powder to gain revenge on a lover.

Located at the center of the market, the snack bar is the place where all the scrap carriers, the fig carriers, the rice carriers, and the taxi drivers stop. Dealings, machinations, wholesale, retail: anything is possible, so long as it pays, by way of small profits or astronomical margins. It is the head office of illegal money changers (CFA francs or French francs, dollars, and even rubles), a must-visit for small-time retailers who pass on their contraband products, but also for pickpockets, with their piercing eyes and nimble hands, carrying out their crimes under the eye of gendarmes or fraud inspectors, who are themselves corrupt. My father tells me that there are undoubtedly some Russian spies going around and

American liaison officers keeping an eye on things: double agents, shady agents, spy, espy, espying, intel, intelligence, intelligencers. I remember all these words that are similar and combine so well together for Scrabble, and without me clearly understanding it, an idea takes form. If in all the markets of the world, buying and selling are the key words and the basic operations, thanks to the N'Djamena market, I understand early on that it is *traffic* that is the key word in history: traffic, the only law of the market. And that all the turbulence, the effervescence, the incandescence of the surface movements actually comes from a very powerful store of trafficking, of threats and promises combined, of fear and darkness.

11

I listen. I say almost nothing but I listen, I always listen carefully. I seize information on the fly, I try to decipher the allusions, I carefully store those that I do not understand. I am particularly sensitive to the sound of voices, to their dull or orangey tone, to their power or their thinness, to the way they let in or pass on the breath of life.

Silence is my constant ally. Older people do not distrust a silent child enough. Very quickly, their prudence falls away and their mania for speaking takes over, on all subjects. Names ring out: Habré, Malloum, Goukouni, Claustre … Françoise Claustre, the cloistered Frenchwoman, is easy to remember. I understand that she is a woman taken hostage in the desert by a certain Hissène Habré, a terrible villain it seems, who captures, ransoms, executes …. But, a few months later, here he is becoming Prime Minister! So, overnight, hated names are praised to the sky—and the reverse is true, too. I discover here, in addition to the vagaries of France's African policy, the fundamental inconsistency of human nature, its wheeling and dealing, its versatility. But I really admire the GNT, the Chadian Nomad Guard, a division of the Chadian army mounted on camels. The animals, elegant, majestic, alive, add a touch of nobility to everything.

Without really understanding them, I am interested in political matters. In May 1978, three thousand Westerners were taken hostage in Zaire by Katangese rebels. We follow this in the French press. On Chad, there is not much. On May 19, the Legion parachutes into Kolwezi. Headlines and front pages in French newspapers—and soon movies, reports, documents, cinema …. On Chad, still nothing.

In July and August, it is the date harvest, the period when the nomads flock to the palm groves. On the way to the market with Saleh, we come across a few of them. Many of them are carrying weapons.

To understand things, I realize that you need books. It is at this time that I start to read a lot. Of everything. Anytime, anywhere. At night, during the day, I spend hours and hours reading: it is the only occupation that can make me stop running with the animals, playing with the school children, chatting with Awa and Amaboua, and even keeps me away from my mother.

I particularly like the books of Jules Verne, where the hero overcomes everything thanks to his crazy ingenuity—and I love even more that moment when intelligence is on the verge of turning into madness and then advances intelligence even further. Thus, I have a passionate admiration for Captain Nemo, a prince of hybridized intelligence (he is of Indian origin and of European education), musician, multilingual, passionate about technique, sworn opponent of imperialism, and protector of the shipwrecked. And I make his motto my own, writing it proudly above my bed:

I love only freedom, music, and the sea.

It is Verne who really introduces me to geography, much more so than my teachers, whom I have completely forgotten. On sea, on land, on rivers great and small, from the Earth to the Moon, from the bottom of the oceans to the summits of volcanoes, I follow him absolutely everywhere. I literally dive *in apnea* into *Twenty Thousand Leagues Under the Sea*. Many children my age read Jules Verne. But some quickly pass over the innumerable, interminable pages where Verne builds up the most varied descriptions: animal, plant, mineral species, long lists of fish, classified—as much as dispersed—in genera and subgenera, types and taxa, species and samples …. But this is precisely what I really like in Jules Verne, the crazy setting out of enumerations that are both terrific and scientific, based on an incredible armada of nomenclature: weights and measures, distances and durations, heights and dimensions, figures and sizes, volumes and indexes, codes and combinations …. It is "Jules Verb," as I call him, the power of the verb, with his long sentences that span the worlds.

Motionless, lying on my stomach on my bed, I move at an incredible speed across the breadth of human knowledge: whole universes, as precise as they are fantastic, appear and rise up, transporting me very far on the hurricane of the pages. The gods are hidden under our beds, while we read Jules Verne.

Between childhood and adolescence, readings are often done in an anarchic way and are from very diverse sources. Newspapers, journals, magazines, albums, various publications and even, in a certain way, advertisements, movie posters, cards and portolans, everything is included, carried, raised in the great storm of reading. For my part, if I like legends (the horse that rides a blue turtle, the boy who spent seven years underwater ...), my imagination leads me especially towards adventure novels (*The Mysterious Island*, *Treasure Island*, and my favorite: the magnificent *Moby Dick* ...). I especially appreciate the stories that portray a child on the edge of several worlds: Tarzan of course, and all his flock of clones, in novels, films, or comics. Tarzan, the ape-man, Akim, the leopard-man, Zembla, the lion-man, Mowgli, the wolf-child, Rahan, the son of wild prehistory .... Beings between humans and animals, impulse and reason, strange hybrids in which instinct and intelligence are one. They are naked and powerful. They belong to several orders, several regimes. They are both lords and savages who speak several languages, including the animal language. Essentially solitary, they find joyful, carefree, and funny companions on their way. Righting wrongs, they defend the weak and the oppressed, always on the side of freedom. They are the heroes of my childhood.

But recently other figures both darker and more realistic have appeared: around the age of ten, I first read *Roots* by Alex Haley, which has just been translated into French, and especially *Black Boy* by Richard Wright. I note there a new fact, which fills me with joy—and, without denying them, will gradually move me away from the naiveties of my childhood: the protagonist is a black man.

*

It is also at this age that what I consider one of the most important events of my life happened: the discovery of music. And, more precisely, playing it. As far back as I can remember, I've always listened to music. But it was in Chad that, for the first time, I started to play it.

Mr. Coulomb, the music teacher, is a stocky and shortish man: his flesh is white, soft, flabby, he blushes easily, the slightest ray of sun transforms him into a copper pot. He looks a bit of a noodle, if he even looks like anything: his livid complexion, the slightly pasty consistency of his cheeks and the vague color of his forehead make him an absolutely ordinary being, remarkable for his very banality. His fragile skin requires constant attention: he is obliged to cover it with damp cloths and constantly dabs his face with a small square white cotton handkerchief. Despite this, he only has to be exposed to the sun for a moment and carrot patches appear on his cheekbones and his ears become two huge currants. His nose swells and is covered with black dots, like a strawberry. On top of this human vegetable patch is some ugly gray hair. Finally, contrary to what his name indicates (and this contradiction pleases me, I who already like to play with names), Mr. Coulomb does not have a *cou long*, a long neck. On the contrary: he has a broad, short neck, sunken into his shoulders, a bull's neck covered in pork rind. And it was from this thick, stocky, full-bodied little being that I took my first and my most wonderful music lessons.

It was my mother who wanted me to play music. For her, who had had a miserable childhood, a musical education was, so to speak, the audible and melodious proof that her child's life would be happier than hers: from this point of view, she was not mistaken. From that moment, music has been the most euphoric thread of my existence. My father, coming from a family of musicians, had no objection, quite the contrary. There remains the question of price: the piano is too expensive, as is the violin. The guitar is more accessible, but cumbersome. The most practical and economical solution is therefore the flute, the recorder rather than the side-blown. So, I opt for the flute.

The word *flûte* itself fills me with delight, with its insolent circumflex accent which gives it an exquisite air. It expresses a certain casualness, a deviation from obligations, a lightening all the more powerful for expressing itself in a simple monosyllabic exclamation: "*Flûte alors!* Blimey!" Classes are held in the evening, when school is over, when the constraints of the day drift away and the night rises.

I remember my first music lesson very clearly. It is evening, the sun is going down, I have my flute in my bag, I go into the house where the teacher is waiting for me. Mr. Coulomb has a disability and cannot turn his head without fully rotating his chest and shoulders, just like the turret of a tank. So, he always stares straight ahead of himself, planting his eyes in my big glasses, like he literally has me in his firing line. The lesson starts right away, with no messing about. Mr. Coulomb swears all the time, he is an old-fashioned pedagogue, he is not afraid of insults, which he mixes curiously with poetic phrases:

"Idiot! Hold your flute properly, that is how you will get the best sounds out of it! Whether it is carved from a mighty bull's tibia, or from a slightly trembling reed ...."

When the last of the sun's rays come in through the curtains, he sponges himself frantically but, in a few seconds, he is crimson. To top it off, his falsetto voice is particularly unpleasant: he speaks through his nose, rising easily to the high notes, giving each of his instructions an air of sour and discordant fanfare. But who cares: soprano, tenor, bass, German fingering, baroque fingering, he imparts to me amongst all the swearing an impeccable technique, punctuating his directives with memorable curses, emphasizing the correctness of the tone and the finesse of the *fingering*:

"Music theory, fool! Music theory! Hold the rhythm! Thanks to the rhythm, you will be able to make the alligators dance to your wooden flute ...."

Finally, as a piece ends and he is happy with me, suddenly calmer and as if pacified by the tornado of notes he has just set free, he turns with all his corpulence to the left, performs a full rotation and looks me straight in the eye. Then, placing his finger gently on his mouth, he signals to me to shut up—to me who never says anything anyway—and for once he smiles at me. I understand then that music continues to be written, even in the silence that follows it.

Music brings the world around me to life and makes it vibrate, making it tangible in a different way. My faculties of perception sharpen, embrace a larger universe, and I'm starting to feel and look at things in a different way. I am enchanted and captivated, the sensations that these first lessons aroused in me would never leave me. The cosmos opens up, the deities return, in a harmonious and fresh language, incisive and alive. This is why every evening, when I go to Mr. Coulomb's to take my music lesson, I have the impression of going to visit the gods of the wind and the sand, the earth and the forest.

The flute changed my life forever. It was with the flute that I learned that a long and rigorous, sometimes even tedious, learning process is necessary to bring to life the most bewitching melodies. With it, too, I understood that emotional treasures could spring forth from a simple piece of wood. The material, the finish, the sophistication of the flute, without being trivial, are not the essential thing: the most humble and coarse instruments can be transcended by technical precision or by the accuracy of the breath—how many times I have noticed that in Africa, and everywhere else. The simple positioning of the fingers on the holes, the rigor of their placement, the suppleness and the dexterity of their variations brought out different sounds, handfuls first then a multitude of notes, and with the notes come the lights, the colors, and finally joy. Only the act of opening up space counts—or closing it, in breezes or puffs of air. Then, the breath passes, the surfaces slide onto other surfaces as they find their volume and depth: the tonic chord.

But Mr. Coulomb is a complete musician. He has lived in Chad for a quarter of a century, he is familiar with the local repertoires. Soon, without abandoning the flute, he introduces me to the balafon. He first gives me a *kundu*, a training balafon, on which I practice on the floor to get used to it. Then he teaches me how to make one: together, we look in the shrubs that line the Chari for a few branches of entada, a very hard, very resistant wood, which we cut into long red bars. Then we place them on long curved calabashes that serve as a resonator. The bars should be thought of as bones in the rib cage, or vertebrae, Coulomb explains to me. The membranes must have a good vibration: bat wings, snakeskin, everything is good, but it is the puffer fish that makes the best resonators, with the skin of its belly firmly stretched. Thus, every part of this red xylophone is in contact with the deities of the waters, of the sky, of the bush.

Then, when he has finished putting it together, Mr. Coulomb tunes the balafon. He spends long moments immersed in extreme concentration, while I observe him in silence and take mental notes of each of his gestures. He hits the bars with short little taps, like a mallet on an anvil. Notes start to rise. Soft, lively, or rough sounds, combined in a unique way, irregular or symmetrical. Everything is in the placement of the sticks, the frequency of the strike and the direction of the variations. Agile intelligence, delight in playing, joy of the balafon.

Finally, when the balafon is ready, I see Mr. Coulomb stand up and begin to dance. He jumps with surprising agility for someone of his build, he has overcome gravity, he is not afraid of the earth. Suddenly he dances and I see his heels kicking up the dust.

12

The child devours the world, swallows it, and gulps it down. He is ravenous. He sucks it in and transforms it by ingesting it. He integrates it into his child's body. But sometimes the world has other ideas. It sends a tribe of parasites into the child's body. Tapeworm, various and vile, anopheles and moths, malaria, filariasis …. A whole plundering and profiteering vegetation which rushes at the body of the child, a crawling and multifaceted aviary, lustrous and scintillating. Burls, larvae, bacteria, slippery shadows whose life is as silent as death. As blind as moles, as deaf as crickets, mute like vipers, they bite and proliferate. Thus begins the dominion of fevers.

With fever, the night is not a simple break between two days, but a kingdom strewn with dreams, sounds, and dread. First, the lanterns light up, the temperature rises, these are the first shivers. They warn us: something is happening, moving, crawling into the depths. The caretaker speaks in the yard, he is making his rounds. I see the lilac flowers of the night lights floating before my eyes. The temperature rises at the same time as the day goes down and the wind picks up, making the laundry flap on the washing line, a night curtain against the fabric of the day. The daytime dissolves in the gray, the gray-pink of the foliage under the slow dive of the sun, the silvery gray of the terrace and the river, the gray-black of the growing shadows: you feel the fever fall on your shoulders like a piece of cotton, which soon envelops your whole body in a burning, untouchable mist.

And then you tremble. You tremble like the poor little lizard in his bare skin, like the infant bitten by a mason wasp. You are hot, you are cold. The fever rises and falls along your limbs like a swarm of ants. Something is digging and climbing, piercing and deepening, gradually shaping its nest, and there is nothing you can do about it. You hear the twilight beasts move, each with its own scent: the brief triple call of the red-naped larks, smelling of the wet savannah, and especially the buffalo toads, stinking of bulrushes and mud, who weave their interminable song into the tapestry of the night. Suddenly, a snake whistles and passes by like a rope. It is he who brings into the room this certainty that lurked in the surrounding night and that you knew was undeniable: you are sick. The child turns over in his bed and rocks in the night. His body burns like a torch. Women pass, dark rings under their eyes, their faces powdered with millet flour and black smoke. Awa? Amaboua? Dick is on the threshold of the bedroom and he is barking. Then he groans, then he is silent, as if he were overcome by the great silence of the fever. All that remains is my mother's voice now, watching over me like a sentry guard, shrinking and fading away, then in turn dying out.

Then, I am falling.

I fall into the city of fevers, the belly of the dream and its disordered incursions.

First, I am a flat expanse, made entirely of water. Lying in my bed, my being seems to me like a pond, then like a lake, then like a lagoon. While the other children are playing hide-and-seek or blind man's bluff, I hold my breath, for a long time, my rib cage is huge, I am a hippopotamus or a caiman. I'm a Yedina child, come from the "grass people," an amphibian lurking in the marshes and breathing with the aid of reeds. I am the child of the border, of the meeting between the earth and the sea, between the sea and the sky, between air and water. Cold-blooded, bare skinned, I am the border itself, always between two orders, between two kingdoms. My father is black, my mother is white. I am fundamentally hybrid and different. Beyond the limits of the atoll, which vanishes in the blink of an eye, the whole world is waiting for me.

I open my eyes. The savannah, the bush, the desert, everything has disappeared. I am nothing but expanse, and this expanse is expanding, from its center to its periphery, at great speed, in a phenomenal acceleration which makes the very notion of periphery disappear. It is an enlargement, a growing tornado, a hurricane that arises.

Words parade like dreams in front of my huge magnifying glasses. I dream of a multilingual and polyphonic Scrabble, where scraps of Latin and Greek are grafted onto fragments of Gorani and Sar, Kanembu and Masa, Fulani and Hausa. Strange alexandrines dance before my eyes: *Falciparum ovale, malaria vivax* .... Sweating, shivering, stammering, I see words tremble in the room, I fall and polyglot words envelop me, and I then understand that it is the secret of the night, the background noise of the night that no one wants to hear, the howl of the grasshoppers eaten alive, the roasted black ants, and other animals eaten cooked or uncooked.

*

When I woke, it was noon.

Large angels in blue and white (blue dresses, white sleeves) were stirring around my bed.

"Malaria is a parasitic disease transmitted by the bite of the anopheles mosquito, which are rife mainly between dusk and early morning," Doctor Pascal, a Chadian physician, explains in a doctorly way to my anxious mother.

Doctor Pascal may be in his sixties, but looks like a young man despite his white beard and snowy hair. In his tight blue linen smock, he spends his time pushing his little rimmed glasses up his nose with his index finger. He looks like a priest, with his smock tied at the collar, his sing-song voice, and his sententious air. His assistant has a small round head, long frizzy hair, sky-blue eyes, a thin nose, a firm chin, and a straight forehead wrinkled with devotion like a server at Mass.

"Malaria is a disease that has two main characteristics," continues the doctor, "an intense fever that causes incessant tremors and chattering of teeth. And then, in the most serious cases, delirium: this is what explains last night's episode, and the fragmented sentences your son uttered."

"What are the remedies, doctor?" asked my mother, both anxious and relieved by the doctor's explanations.

"The first remedy is the mosquito net, which you will soak in a repellant."

"An insecticide?"

"Yes, that's it, a repellant. Also make sure he wears clothes with long sleeves to cover his skin. The room should be very calm and the shutters carefully closed."

"Especially since this terrible sun can cook you up!" adds the assistant.

"Also avoid all places where water stagnates, empty the cups, the planters, clean the basins ...."

"And the dog bowls!" adds the assistant.

"Are there any medications to take?" asks my mother, who is slightly irritated by all this advice regarding her housekeeping.

"Oh!" sighs Doctor Pascal, looking up at the sky. "There are all kinds: quinine, chloroquine, pamaquine ...."

"Atabrine, plasmoquine, rhodoquinone!" adds the assistant.

"I'm going to prescribe you nivaquine," continues the doctor, adjusting his glasses. "I can also recommend medicinal chocolate for children to chew."

"Chocolate? For malaria?"

"Yes, that's it, medi-ci-nal chocolate" (he clearly detaches the syllables and his voice almost cracks on the final one). "Flavored with orange or mango, it has antispasmodic properties that should not be overlooked. Some children chatter their teeth so hard during the fever that they break them!"

"You have to put a stick of licorice in their mouths during the seizures," adds the assistant.

"And how long will the seizures last?"

"Malaria survived the Roman Empire," says Dr. Pascal grimly, sweeping the air with an august hand gesture like an emperor chasing away a cloud of rebellious mosquitoes. "Everything suggests that there will be no end to it."

His assistant finding nothing to add for once, the session ends with these terrible words.

*

In the afternoon, it is Saleh's turn to visit me. I see his powerful chest framed in the doorway, then he dances in like a sparrow hopping.

"It's a spirit that has come to visit you," he announces to me, placing a bottle of rum and some castor oil on my bedside table. "It wants to eat your soul!"

I wonder why Saleh has brought rum, but I quickly understand: he pours a few drops on his fingers and gently massages my temples, which is indeed very relaxing. Then he soaks a towel with castor oil and puts it on my stomach, placing a hot water bottle on top. Using cotton swabs, he also puts more of it on my nails, hair, and eyelashes.

I become all slimy and greasy, sufficiently so to ward off a battalion of Anopheles. Finally, he soaks a few pieces of cotton and puts them in my ears, whispering a Surah. He also intends to burn my feet with a red and black candle, but my mother comes in at this moment and dissuades him fairly firmly.

"Saleh, when will I be healed?"

"We have to find the name of the person who wants to eat your soul, Toumaï."

Later, he will come back and offer to cover my head with a loincloth and get me to breathe in a bouquet of burnt herbs mixed with boiled roots. This decoction would have the effect, he says, of making me say the name of the person who has been trying for several days to eat my soul.

"Saleh, when will I be healed?"

"There are honey days and onion days, Toumaï. When you have finished crying, the onion days will be peeled and the honey days will start to flow like joy."

Finally, he brings me a protective *gris-gris*, a leather amulet representing a lizard with a huge penis, which he wraps around my neck. A few days later, without being able to work out by which of the remedies—Doctor Pascal's or Saleh's—or perhaps under the effect of their combined powers, my condition had improved considerably.

*

Malaria has a yellow face, the color of the earth or of old lemon. It is a monster which, if not muzzled in time, leaves you, even if very young still, with the wrinkled face of a fig and the look of an old man. Whoever goes through the wringer of malarial fevers comes out crushed and forever transfigured, under the guerrilla warfare of mosquitoes. We get sick, we shake, we die. A deadly mechanism which for centuries man has failed to control, or even keep in check.

On at least one point, Dr. Pascal was right: malaria lasts a lifetime. Saint-Malo, Puget-Ville in Provence, Tokyo: over time, the attacks become less frequent, but the monster is there, on standby, and even so many years later, I can still hear in my ears the fantastic battles carried out by the tireless mosquitoes and the zealous bumblebees of nivaquine.

Every now and then, no matter where I am, the fever returns. Headache, muscle pain, sickness, vomiting …. And immense hallucinations. You then have to close the doors, the windows. I withdraw very far under the sheets, the blanket. I bring it up to the level of my eyes, which keep watch in the room for the colored streamers, the mosquito-devils come to bite me and torment me. And there, all night long, I search among the people I have recently seen for the name of the one who wants to eat my soul.

13

An event that could be described as premonitory occurred in early February. It is midday. The heat enslaves the whole courtyard. Dick the dog is peacefully seated in front of the gate. He is completely black, with this red spot in the middle of his forehead which makes him look like a cyclops with a bloody eye. His sharp and shiny fangs stick out over his lips. He is scary. Saleh has just plucked a chicken and Dick is sitting among the feathers. We know that it was not he who created all this carnage, but he reigns there. He is a fierce beast.

Sitting in a corner of the courtyard, in the flat shadow of a banana leaf stuck to the ground by the heat of the sun, I watch the scene and, from the lofty heights of my eleven years, in the shade of my plant, I meditate feverishly on the destiny of humankind. Because I am well placed to know that it is not Dick who is responsible for this massacre. In truth, I am the only guilty party here. The wild beast is me.

*

It is almost eleven o'clock on this February morning when the drama begins. The heat falls vertically onto the yard, a vertiginous furnace that beats down on everyone under the sun, pigs and people, beasts and branches, in a silent torpor, to the point of exhaustion. The heat falls from high up in the skies, then it rises again to the tops of the trees and the rooftops, burning them some more and dissolving them into the fiery day.

It is not the kind of heat you see in a business flyer or an advertising brochure, like you see in the travel agencies that offer tours of Africa. The soft touch of the sunrays that you see in the tourist brochures has nothing to do with this weighty sun, that is dull and unshakable, and fixes in its place every burst of foliage, down to the smallest blade of grass. It is a warlike sun for the suffocating period around noon.

In the midst of this immense stupefaction, Saleh goes about his business as if it were nothing. But he is worried. Several times, he walks in the direction of the henhouse, stroking the necks of the young goats with his hand, then he goes to see my father, who is repairing a sink behind the house. Dialogue, endless chatting, confabulations ... I see the both of them busy together, at the back of the courtyard, in the dry heat. My father approaches me, he explains. One of the roosters is sick: he has pituita. Saleh has to go shopping at the market, I have to help my father look after the poultry.

Pituita is a small callous which grows on the tip of the tongue of poultry and prevents them from feeding: the skin of the tongue becomes rigid, it is like a cartilage which covers it. However much the rooster may try to peck or take a drink, the seeds and water slide over the fine white film that covers the tip of his tongue, fall back into the dust of the yard, and no longer reach his throat: especially in this time of great heat, the animal dies in a few days, from hunger or thirst.

There is only one solution: open the bird's beak and, using a fine point such as the tip of a pen slipped under the tongue, with a sharp blow, as you would to pick a lock, knock off the piece of skin, in order to restore to the muscle its natural flexibility.

But for that, you have to catch the rooster first.

*

He runs away, he flaps, he breaks through the circle of officiants and onlookers, he turns around and faces us, his comb erect, his neck swollen, his wings set for battle. The rooster does not look like he wants to play ball. Awa and Amaboua laugh their heads off. The caretaker sits in his long djellaba, having decided that he will not interfere. Dick and Sao bark like crazy. They are kept away for fear that they will take a bite out of the rooster, or else they themselves keep their distance for fear of being targeted by a fighter even fiercer than them.

A rooster is a ball of feathers and muscles. At the ends of this ball, there are formidable angles and points: a sharp, cutting beak; tapered, tearing claws; a thick, hard comb. And, on the back of the shin, a terrible spike that pierces and tears everything that comes within its reach: the spur. Uncompromising and exuberant, tenacious as well as taciturn, the rooster offers this marvelous combination of violence and lightness to all those who come a little too close.

After several unsuccessful attempts, accompanied by fearful laughter and loud cries of dread, the caretaker gets up and, with a broad and simple gesture, an extension of his arms, wedges the rooster into a corner of wire mesh, protecting himself from the animal with the folds and fabrics of his great djellaba. Then, with a slightly disdainful air of the one who has prevailed without great difficulty where nobody else dared to tackle it head on, he ties up the rooster and puts him in my arms, under the gaze of my father who, as a good soldier, now that the scouting party has done its job, grabs a long, thin needle from a sewing kit and in turn prepares carefully for combat.

Now the plan is simple. We must:

—Hold the rooster.

—Open his mouth.

—Pinch his tongue and pull it out.

—Finally, with a pin slipped under the tongue, detach the callous that stops him from drinking.

We need to do all this while preventing him from biting us, scratching us, slashing us, blinding us, and other pleasures. What could be simpler?

The sun is almost at its zenith now, setting the whole scene ablaze, the father and son on the terrace, sitting on a stone bench in the sun, the overheated chorus of the curious onlookers all around, caught between excitement, laughter, and encouragement. I hold the cock tightly between my two arms, I feel his chest against mine, his talons that plow my thighs, his spurs that scrape my ribs, in an aroma of eggs and flying plumage, acerbic shouts, a big rustling of feathers and cackling in the tragic drama of the day.

A harsh light pierces the tight straw of the shrubbery. The wind sparkles in the sorghum of the fencing, the shade of the acacia trembles, all it can do is tremble, curl up ever more under the crushing sun. It is the hold of the sun, which leaves everything trembling. The rooster is in my arms, he trembles too, ruffled as if he had just got out of bed. I feel with my thumb its neck under the skin, which gives way beneath my touch. On each side of the beak, the barbels quiver, scarlet with anger. His fixed and furious eye looks at each of us in turn with exasperated acuity. My father tries to hold his beak open to remove the callous, but he swells his throat and retracts his tongue, escaping from each flick of the needle with a cutting warbling sound.

"Hold him! Come on, hold him will you!"

I hold him. But he slashes my thighs and grazes my chest. His head bobs right and left, his huge eye open and furious.

"Hold him tighter!"

I hold his skinny neck more and more tightly under the feathers, the reality of life: it palpitates, it is afraid, it is fragile. I see the look of the rooster, his crazy look, his metallic eyes, as if he were trying to be as piercing, as fine, and sharp as the needle whose pricking he dreads. His head goes back into his neck, his wings rustle, his spurs protest, his beak jabs and jabs again constantly. I am literally sawing his neck now, as if my right hand was a knife and my left hand was a butcher's board. All around me, it is as if the heat is being fanned by fear.

"Hold him still! Stronger!"

He's tough. I hear my breathing like a motor in the cabin of my chest. And I also hear the cockerel droning, his bemused complaint of reverberating cackling, an increasingly muffled lament mixed with comic squeaks from below, and on the surface, abrupt, breathless, and hurried cries. My throat is dry, I can feel in my mouth the taste of the pebbles and stones that I picked up the other day in a riverbed. I am the rooster, I have pituita, too: will they open my mouth and scratch at my tongue? And the rooster's eye is still watching us.

Little by little, just as the sun wears the landscape away, the rooster begins to weaken. His eyes roll, his beak opens wider, he searches for something that resembles the air we breathe. Me, my body is in water, the sweat of a wild beast in this stifling heat spread over the feet, the plants, the terrace, and the roofs. My thighs are bleeding, long red ravines on my legs scratched by the madness of the rooster. Suddenly, his head turns and his eye dilates, a full turn as he stares at the circle of curious onlookers gathered for his ultimate rescue. The rooster's gaze wavers and his pupil turns: he must see the red of the courtyard and the green of the fences, and the splendid orange of the hut's walls lit up by the sun. He feels the heat everywhere, so huge and so sweet. Upside down on the ground, he sees the birds flying, and everything on earth is in its place in the circle of the court, dogs are dogs, pigs are pigs, humans are humans, but the rooster itself has already started to die and it is like a secret that opens up in his baleful look, while in my hands the trap closes over again.

Scrabble

*

It was his head that ended up flying off.

I held him so tight, I was so afraid. In one last jump, the body escaped from my hands and ran belly to the ground in all directions, as if looking for its own head. An insane stampede, under cries of laughter and fright greeting the death of his spread-out wings. Then finally he collapsed in a corner of the yard, shook some more, jolted a little, then seemed to drift off, but no one dared to go and look for him, not the children, the adults, the dogs, and especially not the women, who uttered loud cries covering their open mouths with their large hands.

*

Light and sun are everywhere and give the scene a tragic clarity. I crouch under my banana leaf and think. I had killed.

Of course, I had already seen an animal slaughtered many times, the blood of the sheep on the iron spikes, a throat slit. But for the first time, I had taken a life. For the first time, I felt time go up vertically and come down in a single strike, dropping upon us at full speed, the uprooted force of the void when the head falls, the long sense of vertigo that follows this revelation. And above all, I saw for the first time the deathly dress that is worn by beauty. Its exhausting splendor. A power so poisonous that it is better to keep it at bay, for as long as possible, to not try to explain it or even to fight it, just turn away from it to better keep it in check.

"The sun and death cannot be looked at in the face": I remember these words written in white chalk on the green board by the teacher, which I didn't understand at all. Now there is no more refuge on Earth, just the flat fury of the day. There are no more secrets, everything has been exposed. Everything is abolished in the light. The clear and regular universe of the yard (the regulated ballet of animals and people, the shimmering spectacle of street vendors, the graceful choreography of millet threshers) has given way to a fierce universe, a delirium of feathers and blood in front of the gravel huts. You can no longer find there anything sweet and calm, fine or tender. The caretaker picked up the animal's body, then Saleh plucked it when he returned from the market. Tomorrow we will eat it. In the meantime, I remain there under the rumbling sun, the fine and now useless needle like a reed in my hand, in the heat that has no end.

THE WAR

14

Childhood: time passed, the years followed one after the other, traversed by the cries of birds, bursting with papayas and mangoes. Races in the city, reading in the bedroom. Each day piled up on the preceding one, superimposing and multiplying the joy of living, running, and learning, like a leaf placed upon leaf in the bush of the courtyard or on the book table.

Time was passing and we didn't know it.

Everywhere you went in the country of my childhood, there was waiting. There were the stone men, seated on the ground in front of the hut. They drank tea, ate dates or guavas, knocked their clay pipes against the iron pan, chewed cola nuts. They were motionless and they were patient. There were the leaf women, broad, green and plump, shiny, gently round and curved. They stirred a spoon in the clay cauldrons or pounded the bark, tilted the saucepan to keep an eye on the cooking, added a little water from the bottom of a jar. They calmly leafed through every hour of the day. And then there were the river children, of which I was one. Sitting on the edge of the Chari, they stared into space at an imaginary point, munched a piece of banana or a crust of bread, from time to time rising and rushing down to the river, making a torrent of laughter, suddenly flowing over the surface of the Earth.

A whole country in waiting, hoping. We waited for the rain to fall, we waited for the rain to stop. We waited for the meal to be ready at the back of the chipped stove. We were waiting for war to break out, but we didn't know it. Monday, Tuesday, Wednesday. Every day of the week was a different continent. Thursday, Friday, Saturday. I did not see the week as a seven-day link forming a stanza, beginning, work, rest, but as an endlessly renewed series of pleasures and daily observations, at ground level. Tomorrow, the day after tomorrow, hardly existed. Next

week seemed like the end of the world, next month a trip in a time machine. Next year was absolutely irrelevant. Amaboua was right: "Live like a dog!"

However, I particularly remember that day. On that day, February 11, 1979, we left to go outside the city. I didn't know it, but it was to be the last day of my childhood.

*

The only secret is that of the track. The only track is the one straight ahead. Whoever wants to understand a country must travel it on foot or on the track, multiplying the detours or going straight, but always as far as possible.

It is a Sunday in the heart of the dry season. One of those cheerful, sunny Sunday mornings that float like a white cloth or a scent of pastry. The weather is so dry and so hot that my mother has suggested we leave the cauldron of the city to go for a swim in the Chari, some fifty kilometers into the bush, near the Cameroonian border. We have prepared some food, loaded a cooler in the trunk of the car, and we are heading towards the river.

The track is very different to the road. Very different, too, to paths made by human work. The track does not need humans to survive, or his instruments, or his materials. A few herds of animals—the migration of the wildebeest, the whims of the buffaloes—are quite sufficient for its existence or, to put it better, for its survival. Barely used, a track can survive for years. A road is undoubtedly more useful, better marked out, organized otherwise. It will take you exactly where you wanted to go. But only the track opens up in the earth this red blaze which pierces the eyes and traces its savage fissure in the landscape, ripping apart the tamed regions in a thunderous roar, rejecting to the right and to the left the familiar regions, leaving far behind the provinces already known, engulfing them in the dust.

The track leaves the red for a moment, becomes tinged with gray and yellow, with black. The gravel flies up on either side of the vehicle like a rain of seeds rolled and crushed under the wheels and flies back out in a clatter of metal and axles. Forearm stretched out fully, one hand on the steering wheel, you have to put the other on the windshield with a closed fist, from the inside, to exert a pressure point on the window and prevent it from cracking, or even shattering.

From time to time, in the middle of nowhere, we meet people. You can hear them coming from afar, a squeaking oxcart and a few moos. Then we see them arriving, in the powder of the road, outlines and shadows, figurines burned on the earth, escaping little by little. They advance, in their colorful tunics, under their pointed hats or their rolled turbans, accompanied by their carts and all their cohort of pack animals: oxen, zebus or calves, dromedaries .... These are the Bororos Fulani, great cattle breeders. They look at us with suspicion at first. They have followed the line of wells, always on the lookout, watching out for thieves, or cattle traffickers. Then they split their herds up and let us pass, in an orchestra of bells and roars. We are moving close to the beasts, I can even touch them. Their skin is surprisingly fine, mobile, velvety. I feel, I probe .... The muzzle and the underside of the tongue are black and spongy. I also admire the variety of their horns, lyre—or crescent-shaped, bulbous, sometimes rough and striated, or planed down like a stump. I'm learning new words—this word that snaps under the tongue: *cheptel*, livestock. And this other that dances: *transhumance*.

A little farther on, some Tuaregs. The sun strips a man's skin, peels it like an orange, cooks it like a brick. But it can do nothing against the Tuaregs. It can only carve them out, dignified silhouettes, who never bow their heads under its yoke. The Tuaregs are elegance itself. They appear on the horizon, stepping slowly, deliberately, then free themselves along the line of their march, majestic in their bluish fabrics, always seeming to preserve, right against the equilibrium of their bodies, the deep darkness of their tent.

They are warriors, we feel it immediately, through the sharpness of their looks (their keen eyes, sparkling under their scarves), through a certain density in their gestures (the precision of the wrist drawing the gourd). They convoy, they cohort, they caravan— but they never strut around, keeping at all times the discretion of a shadow. The long moving cylinder of the caravan progresses across the mirror of the sands, camels and dromedaries gliding smoothly on the wave of the dunes, in a very gentle movement, smooth and unending. Then their bodies vanish unpredictably, they sink into the great mystery of fire—we turn around and they are already gone.

I remember what Saleh said to me about the Tuaregs: "During the night, they guide themselves by the Pole Star. During the day, a simple pebble or the different shade of the sands is enough for them to know where they are going. Remember, Toumaï: an apparently insignificant stone can be of great significance. A clump of grass can save a life."

"Yes, Saleh."

I have not forgotten.

All these people leaving …. Fate transported them there, between the desert and the savannah, on the neck of an ox or the humps of a camel. They are not exotic figures, on the contrary, they are our doubles and our brothers, they are the very image of our own lives.

It was by traveling along the track that I understood the country a little better. At school, I learned that the territory of Chad was twofold: Northern Chad, a region of grass savannas, steppes, deserts, with a pastoral orientation; Southern Chad, a region of large wooded savannas, with an agricultural orientation. "In the north, they get stuck in the sand, in the south, they get bogged down," said my geography teacher, while my history teacher explained the rivalry between farmers and herdsmen, and suggested an opposition between the "useful Chad" of the South and the "sterile Chad" of the North. By following the track straight ahead, I realized that there was neither North nor South here, nor even the shadow of a country. Chad: a plural, central and radiant, porous territory, at the interface of the Sahara and the Sahel, a wonder placed in the heart of Africa, confusing everything, misaligning everything, tense and shrinking, populated by men from nowhere who leave for everywhere.

Scrabble

*

The Chari, which is the destination of our journey, is also what frames it. It follows us or precedes us all along the track, a whimsical and uncertain companion. In the brightness of this day, its banks smile at us, hidden away under the leaves: the riverbanks play with the bends, with turns of blue and shadow in the red of the track, between the gaps of greenery and the scrambling of birds. The Chari ... I have seen rivers wider than the sea. I have seen the Niger, which is the rival of the Nile. I have seen the Mississippi, with its garland of vowels and consonants and the memory of its black people chased down and bloodied. I have seen the Amazon, which is so powerful that no dam can hold it, no bridge can cross it, and so deep that it covers almost half of a continent. The Chari is not so terrible or influential a river. But I don't of know any that is more playful, more capricious, more charming, more bewitching. It is often said that this wide ribbon of silty water which ripples in the savannah between Cameroon and Chad, catching all of the sun's fire as it passes, is a silver snake crossing the bush. You can see it from a distance, but as soon as you approach it and try to grab it, it scatters and disperses in an infinity of small green islands which break the current of the river and blaze in the sun like diamonds. Sometimes it rumbles and overflows, taking everything in its path, drowning crops, livestock, children. Other times, on the contrary, it offers to all its bands of yellow sand, the freshness of its pools, the hiss of its waters, placid, welcoming.

A wonderful spectacle on the opposite bank, the comings and goings of the elephants, punctuated by the flapping of their ears and the rustling of their tails on the backs of their thighs, their black eyes fixed like two puncture marks on their gray faces. My father sits with me on the riverbank. He teaches me to open my eyes, to prick my ears and to discern, in the jumble of marshy banks, the footprints of animals and the traces of life. The broken branches, the chewed leaves, that mark the passage of the elephants. These round and fleeting shapes that materialize on the blue mass of the river: hippos. Many years later, watching the films of the marvelous Jean Rouch, and in particular *Battle on the Great River*, which recounts a hippo hunt, I will have tears in my eyes before the ingenuity of men and the courage of animals

• 113 •

transfixed in the thickets by the iron of harpoons. But today they are swimming free, their huge muzzles held out over the inverted mirror of the water. A little farther on, there are two antelopes, their bellies half plunged into the river, transformed by the white light into statues of salt, while a lion patiently bides his time hidden in the shadow of a tree stump. Great flocks of birds rise up, draping the skies: the whistling of the ducks and the wild geese drowns out for a moment the growls, the trampling, and the mooing. The sound of the stirred water brings coolness, while I continue to read the magnificent traces of the battles on the ground. Life and death rage in the bushes and under the water of the river.

But the most beautiful spectacle is that of the islands. I descend into the river, as for a last baptism, I plunge into the silt through the fine and lustrous grasses. I feel the fish brushing past my legs and the caress of the *boo*, an aquatic grass that coils around my heels. On the river, the island is a unit of measurement. It allows you to calculate the distance from one point to another, to circumscribe a perimeter, to locate a waypoint. But the floating islands of the Chari take form and move with the wind. They multiply, expand, spread out, join together, and suddenly separate. They vanish, they disappear, they reappear. In the same movement they guide us and lead us astray. They teach us the rhythm of the world, its incessant passage, its grace, and its entanglements. These are "intermittently submerged islands," my father explains to me. They are of all colors: pink or red silica, compact blue clay, white under the acacia petals, golden under the dried grasses. These islands are masterpieces. Delicately wooded or covered with straw, planted with tall grasses, festooned with birds, they leave in their wake a sweet scent of sand and water, as if time itself had evaporated.

Nomadic territories, phantom zones, splendid and shifting islands of my childhood. Between the memories and the colors that intertwine like vines, I see, exactly as when I had dived down there, the submerged shrubs and floating grasses, the creeping stems and the climbing flowers, all the plants that grow by the edge of the water. I hear the mollusks and crustaceans speaking together, I listen to the parleying of the water insects, of the fish, and of the birds. I have learned their language and I can understand it. I can speak it and write it from now on. None of this is forgotten.

15

The heat is intense, the physical and nervous tension is reaching its height. Around us, the greenery slowly disappears like a color that evaporates. Is it the sun that dissolves the characteristics and the limits of each object, giving them a slight ripple like overheated iron? Or is it the drink that my mother pours for my brother and me with a nervous hand, into a white ceramic bowl decorated with two Alsatian storks, which disturbs our senses and dulls them? Are we so focused that everything else goes away? Or else anesthetized by some drug? Only the game board is neat and clearly defined, like a map or a diagram, in the center of the yard, in the center of the table.

Now the grid is gradually closing up, the possibilities are becoming less obvious and are gradually diminishing. The lines are blocked, the words shorten, the best places are taken. The board seems to shrink and no longer allows you to set down your brainwaves. The game is a living organism, an undulating beast of letters and tiles: it has taken off slowly, has fanned out in successive rotations by dispensing its words, combining all the possibilities, opening and unfurling towards the four corners of the table. But its powers are now declining, and it is content to add prefixes, suffixes, onomatopoeias, or monosyllables, awkward subterfuges, miserable ploys. The end of the game is near. A martial eagle observes the last efforts of the protagonists from the top of the tree of creatures. He is indifferent to its outcome: he already knows that there will be deaths and blood.

For most players, the dice are thrown, the last letters are drawn. They struggle to grab a few points on the now overloaded grid, buried under the multitude of wooden tiles become incomprehensible. Only the best players, disdainful of these tricks, know how to find a way and keep in reserve, preferably on a neglected part of the board, a miraculously vacant space where they can slip in a last triumphant, fatal word, even an unexpected series of seven final letters whose meaning would have remained indecipherable until the last tile is added—in the manner of an additional gift or unforeseen grace. But for now, you have to hang on, all senses alert and holding your breath, until the awakening of the kerosene lamps that gradually light up, one by one, trembling in front of the hut, and are the only ones who can still defend it somewhat against the advancing night.

*

Will we ever know where the madness or the fault started? It would be necessary to calculate the share of lies, of false steps, of misunderstandings, to establish responsibilities, evaluate the cowardliness, and add up the complicities. What does a soldier's life in the Chad desert add up to? The fate of a forgotten hostage or that of a negotiator abandoned in the distant dunes? You would have to put everything on the table and empty the drawers, also empty the cupboards cluttered with corpses, whites, blacks, innocent or guilty: money does not have more color than it has an odor. Then, perhaps only one feeling would remain: shame. Shame before the ignorance or the spinelessness of public opinion, of the wars that are nonetheless waged in their name, the trade in arms and votes, all the little arrangements between dictatorships and democracies that have lasted for so long in Africa, between mineral resources and financial investments, the championing of authentic cultures and the continual falsifications, the defense of universal values, and the promotion of special interests.

The images follow on from one another, quickly, sharply. Soldiers everywhere, and everywhere arms—the real source of this tragedy. The weight of the rifles, their heaviness, their appearance at once shimmering (wooded stock) and glazed (metal magazines). For several months already, tensions had been mounting, but we were unaware of it. In July 1977, Bardai had fallen to the rebels. In February 1978, Faya-Largeau. Eight hundred kilometers north of N'Djamena, military planes landed food and ammunition daily on the runway at Abéché airport. The Chadian garrison was reinforced by some five hundred French soldiers of the marine corps, equipped with machine guns. The French aid workers—teachers and doctors—had all already left, evacuated by the embassy, in the face of the support shown by this big agricultural town for the rebel forces. Only one priest, the Reverend Father Damon, had remained in the city. The people of Abéché viewed the French army as an army of occupation. N'Djamena, the capital, was the last hurdle.

War is being prepared, it is about to roll its die. Or else, quite simply, it has already started. As early as 1970 (but I will not see this film until years later), the filmmaker Raymond Depardon produced an excellent documentary, aptly titled *The Ambush*: the film begins at 6 a.m. in Aouzou, in the company of young Toubou revolutionaries, in the ruins of a school bombed by the French air force. One of the first sentences of the film: "We were starting to learn in Paris that there was a French expeditionary force which had been fighting in Chad since 1968. We did not know much about this rebellion, but we would learn later that two hundred French soldiers were nevertheless killed there, without anyone knowing." The war that is beginning still has no name. When it explodes, it is already too late. The war was in its infancy and we were trapped: without our knowing it, the night had filled up with torches, the day with bursts of breeches in the rumbling of rifles.

The "clashes." The "troubles." The "events." Always in the plural, as if to make them swirl in the distance, always coated with confusion and indifference. Not to forget the famous "pacification campaigns," an inverted and false climax. When you hear these words—and a few others, always the same, always different—you will know that you are being lied to and that the war is on.

On Monday February 12, 1979, the day after our trip to the river, a group of students (northerners and Muslim) burst into the classrooms of Félix-Éboué high school and demand that the teachers suspend their lessons. Other students (southerners and Christian) resist, then refuse. Shots are fired. By whom? The striking students? A gendarme wanting to disperse them? In any case, the situation degenerates quickly and the fighting soon spreads throughout the city, opposing the FAT (Chadian Armed Forces) and the FAN (Northern Armed Forces). Régis and I are in high school that day, we hear the gunfire and the clamor, which are like the first rumblings of the murders to come. We are confined to a classroom, with students under the table, the teacher standing, shaking. From under my desk, I can see: her hands tremble, crumpling her blouse. Régis groans: he would like to go out and see what is going on. Very quickly, my father comes to pick us up in the car and locks us in the house with Saleh. Already in the city, war is unleashed: fire, the fire which leaps and crawls, blazes and black smoke. In a few days, the capital will be riddled with bullets and dead bodies, in an indescribable chaos. This is the "first war of N'Djamena," the finally visible beginning of a long hidden civil war.

*

War cannot be retold. It is a dragon that words must approach with great delicacy.

War cannot be retold. One can only evoke its vibration in the bodies of men, its distant and yet inexpugnable tremor. And first of all: fear.

In war everything is replaced by fear. It can be heard first in people's voices. Suddenly, conversations take on an obvious and yet elusive meaning. Unknown realities enter into sentences. The proper names especially, which appear everywhere but refer only to useless certainties or unanswered questions. There is fear in people's voices:

"Habré's forces are trying to arrest gendarmes near the hospital."
"People want to leave for Kousseri."
"The government army has rallied the FAN."
"Where is Colonel Kamougué?"
"Where is General Malloum?"
"What is General Forest doing?"

Suddenly, grown-ups are asking a lot of questions, like children. Scraps of information are gleaned from the mouths and radios around them, each revealing an increasingly threatening, and increasingly incomprehensible, world.

"They say the Sara are fleeing south. We are talking about seventy-thousand to eighty-thousand people. An exodus."

"The inhabitants of the palm groves have fled and taken refuge in the mountains. Thousands of Chadians are crossing the river, by ford or by canoe."

"In the South, Muslims are being systematically executed."

War cannot be retold, but we can see its effects. The mutilation of animals passing in front of the gateway is the first contact with suffering and the absurd. Crippled dogs, sagging hindquarters crushed by the advance of a tank, little goats blinded by the explosion of a bomb ... they stay put, without moving a hoof, their heads hanging down to the ground. Then suddenly they raise their muzzle, their glassy eye looks at you all the more intensely that it does not see you and yet pierces you to the heart.

Now fear lights up all around, burning all day and burning all night.

*

War cannot not be retold, but you hear it and you know that it is war that advances towards you in the inexorable night—because the sounds of war belong only to war.

The impacts of bullet on the ground kick up dust. On roofs, they tear off pieces of sheet metal or concrete. On the windows, they shatter the glass. *Bang bang bang.* All of a sudden, the sounds are filled with disdain: short, low, confined, dense. They answer each other without missing a beat: one, two, three syllables maximum. Heavy, precise, clear. All the minor machine-gun fire of the war, circular, tight, laconic.

And then suddenly, great bursts of gunfire: hidden beneath the bed, where my father has squeezed us in under blankets despite the heat, Régis and I jump like pencils in a pencil case. I hear the roar of big metallic eagles: a mysterious bird has taken over the city, grown-ups call it "Jaguar." They are war machines that fly over the house at a very low altitude and spit huge balls of fire at the ground, roaring as they do so.

The weapons are unleashed. They are the gods of war, its instrument but also, very often, its pretext and purpose. Weapons are the real subject of war. Machine gun, machine pistol, submachine gun, assault rifle, rocket launcher, sniper rifle, grenade launcher .... In a few days of combat, I get to know them by ear, by the sound they make as the barrage begins, but also by the way this sound changes in the air and is transformed according to the nature of the impact, in a stone wall, in burlap canvas, in the bark of a tree or—as I will soon learn—in the organs of a body.

Squatting on the terrace, my father listens and deciphers:

"A 75 SR cannon ... 106 SR cannon ... a 120 mortar ... an 81 mortar ... that's an anti-tank rocket launcher .... Listen, counter-battery fire (75 SR or 106 SR, I can't tell) .... Earlier, they fired SAM7 anti-aircraft missiles, Soviets ... they have a lot of Russian weapons, I also recognized the 76.2 mm anti-tank gun .... And the Kalashnikovs, of course ...."

My father is a living memory of weaponry, an encyclopedia of sounds, portable and itinerant. After a while, he gets up, takes a microphone from his office and walks around the courtyard to record the sounds exploding around the house. My mother tries hard to dissuade him, with no success: it is not every day that we have such an orchestra within reach.

From time to time, we don't care anymore, and despite parental prohibition, we leave the covers and crawl towards the window. Then we get bolder—or get used to it—and we go down to the yard. For the first time, I see the Jaguar bird: a plane all curves and points that rises like a feather, swoops down on the target and unleashes death with an immense grace. Clearance, veering left as it climbs, it sets off again into skies pierced by smoke. One last turn and it has disappeared .... At around 5 p.m. that day, it will once again make several passes, at very low altitude, releasing six and then twelve missiles.

The shriek of a 106 shell rises very high in the sky and then comes back down, passing over our heads. My father listens again:

"The hissing is high-pitched, it means that we are not in its path."

I now know that death is more likely to take the form of a short growl than a high-pitched whistle. As they pass by, each shell stuns us with a resounding explosion like a baseball bat on the head. We remain groggy for a few minutes every time, dazed by the sound.

The gate opens: a neighbor has been injured by an exploding shell. The caretaker lets him in. He is treated with mercuro-chrome, surprised by the depth of the wound. Another was hit by an antenna that fell from the nearby roof, blown up by an explosion. Tongues loosen, panic takes over. The shots are getting closer.

Soon, highly armed vehicles tumble by at full speed in plumes of dust and screams. Cannon Jeeps, with machine guns mounted on the chassis, Toyota pickups armed to the axles .... Our neighborhood is a bit out of the way, but the war ended up finding us. Especially since the house, between the hospital and the morgue, occupies a strategic position, around which the enraged Jeeps turn like crazy.

16

Now the world moves only according to the path of the bullets.

The Jeeps disappear into the rue de Béhagle, a small sloping street that passes by the house, while a column of Toyotas rushes into avenue Bokassa, on the other side. The goal is clear: to take possession of the hospital and the morgue, strategic points where the wounded can be treated and the dead evacuated. In a few moments, the two roads which surround the house are swept by bullets.

Bursts of small-arms fire, then rockets fired into the air. From one end of the avenue to the other, right under my bedroom windows, dozens of trucks fly by at full speed, one up against the other, steel horses spitting their tongues of fire in each other's faces. Is it the sun or indeed death, this fire that blazes on the helmets and the car doors? Man is so afraid that he always rushes to his death screaming. They go on, trying to tear each other apart, firing wildly, wastefully, sparks flying from all sides like carbuncles on bodies. They move on, and it looks like the whole earth is on fire.

The two columns of vehicles come into contact at the crossroads, just in front of the house. The ground groans under their tires as they circle the roundabout at breakneck speed, machine guns firing nonstop from the back plate, a whirlwind of bullets slashing the walls, decapitating the trees. The leaves fly off, the trunks fall down, the bark flies like pieces of torn skin. The branches of the tree of creatures are riddled with bullets, the birds fly away in large handfuls of feathers, the monkeys scurry about, screaming.

At the crossroads, the Jeeps continue to whirl like fireflies caught in a jar, carried away by their circling movement, shooting at and killing each other at point-blank range. A speeding car smashes the edge of the roundabout and overturns, causing the almost immediate cessation of this crazy situation. The others slam on the brakes, in a screech of tires and a hurricane of dust, some overturning as they swerve quickly, crushed bodies, crumpled machine guns, screams and crushing of bodywork. Several vehicles then escape from the trap and go up towards avenue Charles-de-Gaulle, where they come face to face with a tank, the machine gunner bareheaded on its turret, firing in all directions in his gyrating delirium. It is now the machine that controls, shell, track, armor plating, the dry snap of automatic weapons. War takes possession of the world through vertigo, the spinning has gone mad, a crazed machine now obeying only its own stubbornness and responding to nothing.

Soldiers have taken refuge in the carcasses of the overturned vehicles. They are lying down, firing. They sometimes glance over the charred scrap iron of their makeshift shelter, throw a grenade at random, lost in the gusts of sand and the black smoke of the burning vehicles. A terrible smell of petrol and burnt rubber rises: it grabs you by the throat and stings the eyes. Between two bursts of fire, they look at each other from afar, dumbfounded to be there, clinging to anything that remains somewhat solid in this deluge of noise and fire, an overturned vehicle, a shredded palm leaf, the shadow of a charred shrub.

The more the shots intensify, the more the clamor dies down. Mouths no longer emit words or orders, or even shouts: all they emit is fire. The sound of machine guns resonates dully, in basso continuo. Shooting single bullets, shooting in bursts of three, shooting in random bursts …. At regular intervals, we hear the metallic noise of the breech which slides and turns on its axis to take on again its supply of powder. My father's technical precision at such a moment is mind-blowing: "Six hundred rounds per minute, at this rate, a magazine of 20 cartridges lasts two seconds …. They have ammunition, it will last a long time." And it lasts, yes. They spin, eject, insert, spit, and hum. They kill. It is not so much my memory that has retained the form and content of these noises, but my body. Even today, as I trace these lines in writing, the spitting of the Kalashnikov fills my ears, my eyes, my nostrils, and my mouth. I have forgotten nothing.

Some want to flee. The guard has closed the gate tightly with lots of chains and padlocks: if a soldier tries to enter, we are all in danger. Scenes of hunting and death, right before our eyes. The slightly overhanging terrace offers an exceptionally grim view of their maneuvers. Khaki uniforms hunt down other khaki uniforms, clearing the sidewalks with a submachine gun, searching inch by inch through the entire Bololo neighborhood opposite us, wiping out the fugitives who respond with sporadic shots or scatter into the alleys running fast, like bees emerging from the hollow of a rock.

Shoot, run, run, kill, shoot again, in the foliage, across the cars .... Soon, there is nothing more to shoot, but they still shoot anyway, they even shoot more than ever, as if a mechanism had started and could not stop. All gestures suddenly seem isolated, disconnected from any will and above all from any form of intelligibility. The most absurd actions seem reasonable and the most reasonable actions become absurd, in a strange reversal of polarities. That is perhaps even what best characterizes war: not only all that one does not understand but which suddenly seems normal to you, and even anodyne (a hand torn across its width, to which only three fingers remain attached, dangling in a stream of blood, if it is still a hand), and everything that could seem insane and yet takes on a form of unreal logic (the same hand picking up a grenade to throw it a little farther). Finally, there is no longer any courage, daring, precaution, or prudence: there is only war, and its cohort of gestures both absurd and coherent, clear and disordered.

Bursts of machine guns and cars, which again stop at the crossroads with all doors open and slamming, loud speakers declaiming. These are the reinforcements. The situation seems to calm down when a van loaded with gasoline containers explodes. Then the pickups move on towards other yells, carrying death everywhere with them.

Leaning on the window, having left the bed and the blankets behind us, I watch with Régis the mad disarray of men. All senses on the alert, I am attentive to the innumerable trajectories of the gunfire bursts. Fugitives fall under all kinds of bullets and it is always the same death. But each bullet has its route, its singular trajectory: it seeks the corner of a door, the leafy tops of a tree, or the roof of a building, but all along its course, it can fork off at any time, opening a degenerate space that is the very definition of war. War always spins out of control, always. The victims are never collateral, they are at the very heart of war, blunders are the very ink of war, its clearest signature—and the child sitting on the ground in the dust smiles a strange grin as the bullet finds his neck.

She runs, the neighbor runs, she shoves people, shouting.

"Let me pass, he's my son!"

She trembles, her hands tremble when she picks up what is left of the child, as she tries to put it all back in order, the pieces of bone and the fragments of his skull, as sharp as shards of earthenware, all the glassware of her son in the dust of the sidewalk. She is trembling, her lips tremble when she tries to say something as she hugs the child's head to her chest, but a word or letter is still missing. She is trembling, her eyelids are trembling, but she has lost her only son and can no longer cry. It's the last scene and it's the last salvo. A sniper stands on her right, rocket launcher on his right shoulder. He puts his left knee on the ground and adjusts calmly. A huge blast crosses the street, a large orange flame: the van behind the woman is lifted up by the blast of the impact and falls on her in a cloud of debris and dust—from which I see her coming out, crawling on her hands, her child still in her arms, the woman with her face bloodied and both legs cut off.

This is the last scene I can remember, before my father chases us, screaming, towards the bed and slams shut the bedroom window.

17

I was lying on my bed, a book in my hand. For the past week, my bedroom had been protecting me, trembling as it shielded its simple and fragile coolness from the tumult of the day. My book also protected me, a refuge of paper among the surrounding carnage. My brother was sleeping peacefully beside me. The afternoon sun was filtered behind the almost closed shutters, where a flicker of light was glinting, blinking gently from yellow to orange and from orange to bronze, like a glittering butterfly placed between the glass and the wood.

Everything was calm, motionless. My mother had prepared this drink for us, an infusion made from Indian-apple leaves, and we could sleep now. I had entered a beautiful clearing, wide and round like the yard: the caretaker's hut, the two dogs crouching in front of the gate, Awa and Amaboua having fun and laughing near the fig tree in the background. I never left my bed or my book, lying in the shade of the room, my eyes fixed on the shimmering light.

Through the slit in the shutters, I see a bird approaching, walking on the windowsill, the spiky feathers, and the flapping wings. I recognize it immediately by its large gray collar. It is one of those who usually nest on the banks of the river and is called the "ruff." His belly is white, his lower back and tail have black dashes. He pushes the glass with his long, pointed beak and enters the room very slowly. Is he the ghost of the rooster? His collar swells and he heads for me: suddenly, ruffled with anger, he gives out a mad scream, opens his wings, and is about to attack. It's the mating period and he's trying to devour me.

*

I wake up in my bed, bathed in sweat, but this time it's not malaria, it's not the sweat of a fever and it's not a nightmare either. Or rather, the nightmare has come into my very life. I definitely heard a wild howl, preceded by great bursts of submachine gun fire. I rush to the window and look out into the yard.

The table in the center of the courtyard, on which we used to play Scrabble, has exploded: there are shards of bullets in the wood.

The caretaker's hut has also been blown up, struck by a grenade: its exploded rectangular form now has the shape of a star. Pieces of straw hang from the roof and have started to burn. And before it a shadow, armed with a rifle.

The yard has become a large, useless chessboard where, calmly, two child soldiers hold us at gunpoint.

Armed soldiers have entered the yard, the yard through which everything enters, and all kinds of shadows now weave their way through the palisades, rifles slung over shoulders. They come in, and within seconds they tear up the book of my childhood.

*

A man shouts, he will soon die. A man laughs, he will soon kill. So that's what war is, this foolish, mocking laughter.

The soldier is very young, a few years older than me, perhaps sixteen, seventeen at the most. He killed Dick first, who was threatening to bite him, a bullet between the eyes, right where the red spot was, above the muzzle, in the middle of the forehead. Now he stands next to the caretaker, who nevertheless tried to hold the dog back. After some chatter, he again takes out the pistol from the holster attached to his belt and places the end of the barrel where the throat meets the chin. I understand the expression "point blank," which I have read so many times in books. There are many kinds of wars. And here, it is war within war. An execution. It is both the fastest and the slowest of deaths. He has his index finger on the trigger and he's going to shoot.

Killing: it is a simple gesture of the arm, I realize. Nothing easier than to kill, at least after the first time, you can even do it with a smile on your lips or while thinking of something else, with a kind of indifference or a little furtive pleasure, like sliding a zipper up and down, like undoing the buckle of a belt. We get used to everything, we sometimes end up liking it (the unmistakable sound of the metal piece sliding under the bolt, the frightened look of the victim which gives a slight feeling, fleeting but intense, of omnipotence), and then one day we also probably get tired of it—I understood everything about war, I understood everything about death and murder when I saw someone kill for the first time. It's a huge useless revelation, the pleasure of killing.

The gun goes off, and the head tumbles in a cry. I remember perfectly the movement of the facial muscles when the shot was fired, as if extracting all the hatred, an old store of ancient terror, a constipation of all the mayhem. The caretaker's head flies backwards and is almost entirely stuck on the wall of the hut, bits of brain, cartilage, hair and teeth, the pulp of the lips, the bones of the skull and the nose, the blood.

The young soldier reloads, grabs the caretaker's son by the shoulder—he must be his age—and puts him in the same place where his father just died, and he shoots a second time. Nothing is more repetitive than war, more haunting and more singular each time. In war, everything always takes place at least twice, as if it wanted to make sure that we understood correctly, that it is it that reigns, that it will do what it wants, that the most absurd of acts may, under its control, be committed as many times as it wishes.

This time, only the jaw is shredded by the pistol shot, the top of the face is whole and intact above the bloody mouth. The boy holds his head in his hands, as if to prevent it from exploding. The pain follows its course through his body like a red, devouring missile. By the time the information gets to his brain, his eyes go up to the sky and his whole body suddenly whitens. He literally sees himself leave, his face chewed up by death. He can't even howl, his jaw is on the ground, he already sees nothing but the insane stupefaction of his body departing, the immense surprise of his own death.

*

What is war? Combat, and much more than combat. It is violence, but also something other than violence. It is conflict and conquest, but for whoever experienced it, it is much worse than that.

Later, throughout endless courses in literature, philosophy, anthropology, and political science, I will learn that a certain idea of language and of relationships is lost in war, that it occurs precisely when language no longer allows men to be reconciled and settle their differences. But there is something else, something deeper and more vital, that I saw in the yard that afternoon. War is always there. In peace as in war. It is just that there are times when it resurfaces and you understand then that it was there, but that you did not know it. The belief in the goodness of men, in their *human* nature, that is what war destroys when it emerges, very quickly and almost effortlessly.

War is a voracious flower, a carnivorous plant. War is furious like the night and like the night you cannot understand it. All attempts to classify it are futile. Cold or hot war, civil or planetary war, war of liberation or war of religion, maneuver warfare or trench warfare, world war or guerrilla .... But it is nothing other than the deepest part of man resurfacing, his very reason for being there: immense, massive, and monotonous war, this enormous disaster which goes back to the beginnings of history and will not stop.

There was so much blood in the yard that it had to be washed down with water. Awa and Amaboua took care of it, rubbing the blood of their executed father and brother from the trellis of their burnt-out hut. They weep, and the whole hut is a tomb, the mother of sorrows. The tap in the yard is leaking. This discreet but regular noise becomes maddening, unbearable over time.

I was lying on my bed, a book in my hand. It was war that came looking for me.

TCHAD

14.2 85 Valentin

Le général Malloum demande un cessez-le-feu... et des armes

APRES l'appel au cessez-le-feu lancé dimanche soir par le général Félix Malloum pour que s'arrêtent les combats opposant dans le nord du pays forces gouvernementales et rebelles du « Frolinat », une certaine inquiétude règne à N'Djamena.

Depuis le début des hostilités, le 1er février, les autorités sont restées relativement discrètes sur l'évolution des opérations pour dégager Faya - Largeau et Fada. Mercredi dernier, le chef de l'Etat tchadien avait dénoncé « une offensive militaire de grande envergure » lancée par la Libye contre son pays et avait demandé « une aide militaire conséquente » à tous les pays amis du Tchad pour faire face à cette situation. En réponse, le président égyptien Anouar El Sadate a affirmé que son pays continuerait à soutenir militairement le Tchad.

Les observateurs notent que la volonté exprimée par le président Malloum de réexaminer la plainte adressée par le Tchad contre la Jamahiriya au Conseil de sécurité, si d'ici au 16 février le cessez-le-feu devient effectif, marque la volonté des autorités tchadiennes de faire un ultime effort pour établir le dialogue avec Tripoli.

Otages :
Croix - Rouge et chefs musulmans
possibles médiateurs

De son côté, l'oncle du jeune otage français Christian Massé, le père Houdry, a rencontré hier des représentants de la Croix-Rouge nigériane qui l'ont assuré de leur coopération pour obtenir la libération de Massé et de son camarade suisse André Kummerling.

Le père dominicain s'est d'ailleurs rendu hier à Ibadan pour tenter de rencontrer l'évêque de Maiduguri (ville nigériane la plus proche du Tchad).

Selon le résultat de ses discussions, le père Houdry se déclaré prêt à se rendre au nord-est du Nigeria pour essayer de rencontrer des chefs religieux musulmans proches de la zone de détention.

18

Life had left us there, between the hospital and the morgue. For a week, we lived like this, in the whistling of bullets and the roaring of the Jaguars. Empty cans and water bottles were piling up in the house. Occasionally, long lulls made the wait for the next burst of gunfire even more unbearable, and you could not know if it would be just a skirmish or the start of a bombardment. We had to go back into the bedroom, slide under the bed and pull up the covers, "without making a sound," my mother curiously specified, while the whole world was exploding all around us. One raging day followed after the other and only the early evening brought relative calm, peppered with shells and tracer bullets, but which nevertheless allowed you to catch your breath. Time seemed to have coagulated around the house.

Sleep, even the deepest sleep can no longer save you from such carnage. I remember very clearly the decision I made that Saturday evening. The night is falling slowly, the road in front of the house is disappearing into the mystery of the evening. The sunset lights the whole terrace on fire, then suddenly the red sun drops behind the tops of the trees and everything turns black. Children, are you afraid at night? No, children are not afraid of the night, they are afraid of the war that is at the heart of the night. The night of war is never light and subtle: it is thick and dense. It is a heavy fever that floods the streets and drowns the huts. So, night adds on to night, and after a while all that remains, placed at the bottom of the night like a faint lantern at the end of a dark alley, is a yellow point that crackles from the other side of the boulevard, itself also engulfed in shadow. A fire burns in the Bololo, catching my eye.

War, at the worst moment, is silent like a corpse. On wartime nights, the birds no longer whistle. Everything stops. And even the dogs are strangely silent. Awa says that Ni-kolo, the spirit of the dead, moves around at night, and that it ignites fear in the hearts of children. I'm going to follow Ni-kolo then, and I'm going to show him that I'm not afraid, since everyone has been telling me for a week: "Children, don't be afraid—Don't worry—It will stop soon …." That evening, like every evening, my father turned on the radio. "The radio station is on fire," the radio announces. The world seems to have gone crazy, when the airwaves themselves tell you that they are going to die.

So, I go out. I adjust my glasses, I take my knife, and go out. No force can stop me now. I head for the hole in the fence, behind the banana trees, I go around the hut. At the same time, gunshots can be heard, then a quick succession of bursts and, in the dark there are high-pitched cries which rise up like spears. I hold my breath, I grab my knife and, in my turn, I enter into the night.

*

Outside, the air tastes like hot metal.

Tracer bullets whistle above my head, digging their phosphorus furrows into the night, like giant matches that light up everything nearby. The next instant, the city plunges back into darkness.

I run across the boulevard and confidently enter the Bololo. I see the fire pulsating over there, I am determined to reach it. Over-excited men march and threaten, they are in boots and armed, but in the general excitement, they do not pay attention to an eleven-year-old boy grazing the walls. The flames of the fires spread over the huts and sculpt their frightening figures there: as soon as you spot them, they disappear. Flashlights turn on and off. They have genuinely huge boots, which stand out in the glare of the embers and which, with the lighting, rise to head height, just like the ogres in the folk tales.

I stumble, but I move on. On the ground, rickety crates and bags of shredded canvas, sawn trees, branches thrown to the ground between planks and foliage, long gourds and round gourds, empty barrels. Here a dented machine gun, whose barrel is tangled up in a tree, sits in a small square. There the remains of charred Jeeps thrown on their side. Almost everywhere, little islands of waste. The buildings, riddled with bullets, have lost all meaning: they stagger towards the ground, crumble, and collapse into the clay—everything leans towards the shadows. War is a kind of tornado: it swirls in the streets, bores into walls, trees, houses, and even into our very idea of a city.

The earth is shrinking and lies cluttered with corpses. The large strip that looks like a vacant lot—which will later become the Place de la Nation—turns into a narrow tongue, dark, and glaucous, covered with bodies over which floats a gigantic cloud of flies. Their buzzing is so loud that I plug my ears, for fear that they will get into my brain. And then dogs, countless dogs, a pack of dogs that angrily gorge themselves. Snapping of jaws on corpses, the enamel of their fangs at night. The dogs are now as crazy as the men. The dead resemble vacationers lying on the sand, but strangely motionless vacationers devoured by dogs.

I keep on going towards this curious red-and-yellow light that burns in the distance. On the way, I meet only the dead. Or rather: arms, backs, legs, a chaos of clothing browned by blood and purple faces under the khaki harnesses. The cannonade catches up with me as I reach almost to the other side of the neighborhood, towards the mosque. The sound of a heavy machine gun recognizable among all the other noises, the sound of a stampede and a herd. I hide for a moment behind the carcass of a sand-colored pickup. Soldiers pass: they march quickly, they are sweating, hatred shines on their skin. They are swept away by forces they do not control, lost in the delirium of war. They go around the corpses, turn them over, search them, loot them. They roll up the sleeves, empty the pockets, rob the teeth. The dead are lifted and stripped in one fell swoop to recover a shirt or a uniform. A soldier gets up: he burps, and his burp makes an insane noise, the sound of a flayed pig that almost surpasses that of the cannon fire. Then he turns around and his foot approaches the head of the dead man. He strikes, with all his might, several times, with great kicks on the still limp body. Finally, a last kick in the head placed on the ground like a coconut to make sure he is really dead, yes that's it, he's had it, that one.

They kill the dead. They kill them a second time. Sometimes they fire great bursts into already dead bodies, to be sure, once and for all. But you have to save bullets. So, they squat on the man, flat on his back, covered with blood, and with a fierce gesture they draw a big X over his face with two strikes of their knife. I lower my eyes, as if not looking still protected me a little. When I look up again, the little red-and-yellow flame that was shining near the mosque has disappeared. I am terrified, scarified by fear. At that point I know, I know that it is not the night that has covered the world, the world has sunk into darkness.

*

"Toumaï ... Toumaï ...."

I was about to turn around when I heard it.

A groan. Not even a cry or a moan, rather the phrasing of a bird, of weak intensity.

It is a fragile voice, so fragile. But this voice, I would recognize it anywhere. It is Youssouf. He looks as surprised as I do, both amazed to find ourselves there, in the Bololo, in the middle of the night.

He is lying on the ground, his old woolen shirt torn, a hole in his stomach and small bubbles of blood, slivers of which seep through the fabric. He looks at me and his teeth chatter. The noise of the jaws knocking together produces an unpleasant sound on this hot night: you can feel that something in his body has gone wrong.

It's Youssouf and it's no longer Youssouf. His face is unrecognizable. A layer of earth covers it, like a glazing, like a varnish. His beautiful scarifications now look like lumps of clotted blood. On the entire left side, his face is blue, blistered, as if it were going to burst.

"Are you in pain?"

"It's Abdel ... Abdel shot me."

I am stunned. Later, I will understand everything—if anyone can still understand something in this absolute, total delirium. Abdel's visual acuity got him enlisted by the soldiers. We had seen him chatting with them several times and gradually drifting away from our childhood games to enter an adult world, harder and indifferent. In war, the accuracy of a shooter can be very useful. But why did he shoot Youssouf? This is a mystery that I will never unravel.

Youssouf is lying on the ground. A first bullet tore off his temple, from which a greenish liquid now flows. A second came to be lodged in his belly, making of him this little bubbling geyser.

I look at him in shock, even more than pity. Is it really him, this bloody flesh gathered in my arms? All around his left ear, the bullet has cut deeply into the tissue and the flesh is raw. It looks like his skull has been plowed with a spade. Now it is his turn to enter into the darkness.

Beside him, another wounded man, also young, moans like a heifer giving birth. His groans rising into the night take away all solemnity from this moment. I think back to the sheep. The hands on the white coat of the sheep dying in fear is one of the most disturbing things I have seen in my life: they inject both death and calmness. Contact was never broken, until the last moment, with the animal. But man, the man killed in the war, always dies alone, in a definitive solitude.

Slowly, I reach out my hand towards him and I ask him again this pointless question, which does not seek an answer, which is only a way of speaking to him some more, of keeping him among us a little, of accompanying him as long as possible:

"Are you in pain?"

He winces. It is his body that responds for him. He contorts, twists like a worm on a hook.

He whistles a little more, between his chattering teeth.

He scratches the dust, one last time. He dies. I see him trying to trace a last sign in the sand, as precious as it is derisory. A *Y*.

Youssouf, having traced with his finger in his land the alphabet of his own death.

A little later, other soldiers came to look for him. They took him on a stretcher, his face covered in black soil swaddled in a large white cloth. From beneath the folds of the sheet stuck out a huge black bloody toe, big like an ox-eye window. This is the last vision I had of fleet-footed-Youssouf.

Then, I understood that I had come to the end of the road, that I had just touched something black, soft, formless, to which nothing could give shape—not the grace of the dogs on the sand, Saleh's wisdom and his gentle, affable look, long walks in the city, or mornings spent reading, the enchantment of the birds, the long gliding trace of the canoes on the river, not even the musical scrolls of Mr. Coulomb—and that left me alone, stranded in that night. It had suddenly disappeared, life, curled up before my eyes like a bird's corpse which a dog's muzzle shakes and turns before devouring it. In that moment, I felt alone for the first time in my

life. Because it was very clear and apparent then: I had come to
the end of my childhood.

*

The feeling of one who has known war through the body *has
nothing to do* with one who knows war only through images or
reports. I experienced war. Since then, I have worn its mark on the
outside and a small margin of shadow keeps me separate from you.

Why did Abdel shoot Youssouf? I will never know. I can't forget
it, I can't erase it. Nor can I give this act the slightest meaning. That
is war, and war, contrary to popular belief, is never methodically
fought from side to side, it always rages all against all.

War: everything we will never understand. War is the opposite
of childhood: it is that moment when we realize that we have
absolutely no chance of getting the answers to the questions we
ask ourselves. Nothing can be grasped or explained anymore. War
leaves the world to its fundamental incomprehensibility. It is like
the sun: a huge question with no answer.

*

I went home, strangely calm. Régis was not asleep. He was waiting
for me.

"Where did you go?"

"To the Bololo."

"Do you think it's really the right time for a walk?"

"I know."

It was the first time he had reproached me.

The next day, my father made the decision to leave the house. In
Paris, a governmental crisis meeting had already led to the decision
to evacuate the "expatriates" (that word, I never liked it), but the
Chadian capital was cut in half at the cathedral by a line of fire
that was said to be impassable. It was up to each family to find
a way to get to the airport, which was held firmly by the French
army. A French flag fluttering on the left, a white flag fluttering
on the right, we crossed the whole city by car, passing in front of
the Notre-Dame de la Paix Cathedral, ravaged by bullets and still

standing by some miracle. This trip to the north, which I had done so many times on foot, I was making for the last time. From there, a military cargo plane, the Transall, transported us to Libreville airport in Gabon, then to France, Paris.

Epilogue

Very slowly, the child reaches towards the shadow. What will he find there, in the bag of darkness? There are only a few letters left and this is the last move. His fingers shake a little, move, interpose, and displace, patiently staging a final strategy. At that moment, his mind is a kind of musical instrument: tones and modes, groupings, concordances, he looks at the grid and searches for the best possible opening. The chain of places and years is falling back into place, which allows an infinite number of free links and associations, cross-references. Assonances, dissimilarities, resemblances, consonances come back to him in memory, like the pieces of stone in a mosaic, where school memories come together, aphorisms, proverbs and sayings, song lyrics, the great ocean of books, and the complex network of readings.

In the early days of Scrabble, the game always started at the top left of the grid, and reaching the star was the player's goal. It was much later that the star became the starting point. Now, it is from the star that we must always start, the great territory of childhood at the center of the table, the one from which unknown words can spring up and a new game can start.

*

I never left my childhood.

My childhood is a city lost on the edge of the sands, but it still resists everything that attacks, everything that roars and everything that dies, everything that brutally threatens to end. It is there, simply, infinitely distant and yet infinitely available.

We are lines. Or more precisely: we are spirals. Like the spiral, we leave nothing behind as we develop, as we grow. I have forgotten nothing, or almost nothing. As in the spiral, everything is always there, in itself, inside, *within reach*. You have to know how to stay—or become again—a child in order to be an adult, thus passing between the worlds.

The yard, the trees, the windowpanes which become large trembling gold leaves when evening falls, the warm smell of the earth under the caress of the rains, the river, its lapping, the ebb and flow of the water, and that of my reveries, the marvelously slowed-down time of kisses and all the variations of light—broken, crushed, then deployed again—all of this now arises again from the Scrabble board. Youssouf, Abdel, Saleh, my mother, Awa the youngest and Amaboua the elder: I walk between words and the dead and I know now that I have not forgotten anything. Everything had remained buried in me in a very deep region, with the voices that have fallen silent and the tortured bodies.

My heart, my heart beats like a drum, a force pulls me obscurely: I touch the dark depths of my memory, the very secret of writing.

*

Now, as the pages turn, I see things more clearly, and I can reconstruct what happened.

It was my mother who placed us there, in the center of the yard, behind the banana trees, between the gate and the palisade. The place where she says bullets are the least likely to hit us. My mother: ready to leave, ready to do anything to leave this hell, wearing her big black coat like a bag full of worry, in the infernal heat of the yard.

She was also the one who had taken out the Scrabble and asked us to play. A surprising initiative, an incongruous proposal, which might even have made us smile in other circumstances. She had read in a book that the mountaineer Chris Bonnington had taken a Scrabble board to the heights of the Himalayas to fight mountain sickness during the ascent of Annapurna, because this game facilitates concentration. Perhaps it would allow us, too, to think only of the game, amidst the whistling bullets.

I can clearly see once more, on a corner of the table, this open medicine box: unfolded leaflet, shredded cardboard revealing two white pills in a torn aluminum package. These are sedatives, taken out of my mother's vanity case and given to us with a nervous hand. But the drugs are not enough: then Saleh brought an armful of crumpled leaves, from which stick out branches of large white, cone-shaped flowers. It is the Indian apple, a formidable psychotropic drug. In other countries, it is called the *datura*. It is given out to the sick, pregnant women, and those condemned to death: it is also sometimes given to children who are afraid. Poorly administered, it causes violent hallucinations. (This is why, sometimes, I tell myself that I dreamed these scenes, or that I would prefer to have dreamed them.) For an entire week, we will drink cup after cup: this is Saleh's last gift, a drink of madness, love, and forgetfulness, like a form of wisdom for the end of time.

Silence. Silence right to the end of the world.

Children play. Around them, a country collapses. In the sky, vultures and tawny eagles. The vultures have left the grassy meadows, savannas, swamps, and sparse woodland. Those who usually keep away from cities and towns, have settled in the trees that line the house and in the thorny brush. They hover over the city by the dozen. They wait and watch. Raptors hover over our heads and feed on corpses.

Thus, slowly, gradually, inexorably, all the innocuous details of the beginning find their place and the whole picture becomes *readable* again. We hear gusts, but it's not the wind. We hear clicks, but it's not the bedsheets: it is the detonations.

Snipers are posted in the trees; their weapons gleam and you never know if it is the shimmer of the breeches or that of the leaves in the sparkling clutter of the palisades that surround the house and where the bamboos sparkle like embers. The soldiers shoot, they shoot everything that moves. We hear explosions in the leaves. The palm tree covering the hospital with its beautiful green tuft has been beheaded. The gas station is on fire. Sometimes a golden sparkle on the iron roof: it's a sniper falling and swirling like a dead leaf. Another sits at the foot of the same tree and looks like a burnt stump: an exploding shell carbonized him.

"What direction is the wind coming from?" My mother keeps asking the question. The answer takes on enormous importance, because it is the wind that brings us the scent of the nearby morgue, where the dead pile up by the lorry load. Death. No smell more rancid, or more difficult to describe. Death, this catastrophe of smells. Where does the wind go? Where does it come from? The answer is constantly changing and we have to move constantly from room to room to avoid breathing in the scents coming from the street.

Thus, slowly, through the wisdom of my mother, the yard becomes this unexpected oasis, stuck in the middle of the fighting: a refuge planted with banana trees and where we play Scrabble. Scrabble: another way of settling conflicts, intelligent, inventive, calm. Word battles on a revolving board. And a justice of the peace: the dictionary.

All around, it is only weapons that speak.

The yard has become a haunted, untouchable place. Now, we will never again get out of this yard, this wide solitude, this morning cooked and recooked under the sun drunk with rage that turns in the sky, like a huge unanswered question. I already know: I will never leave this courtyard, where we play Scrabble, occupied only with death and words.

But the man I was already and the child I have remained have this in common: at the height of war, when human violence or that of nature is unleashed, they always see words move around in the yard. Words, only words are able to give a precise shape to our anxieties—green landscapes, ephemeral lakes—and to bring to them the beginning of an answer, always precarious and provisional.

Thus, words start over and over again a combat already fought a long time ago. Is there no other word for *house*? We will find another one. Has the word for *patience* already been burned? We will relight another one. Has the word love succumbed to the gunfire? We will resurrect it, recreate it, in other forms, a little later on. And all of this is possible with a single movement of thought, as simple as a wave of the hand. This strange gesture, as precious as it is derisory, is that of art.

In the same way, for all these years, a hidden combat has taken place—strange quarrel, paradoxical alliance—between death and the letters that I trace on the page. Calmly, very slowly, I go down into the words, right to the final darkness where each letter is a silence and where death speaks to us. Now I see *behind* death. Have you ever observed a child walking on a beach and discovering the dead body of a bird? He approaches, he is not afraid, he crouches, lifts the beast a little. But the animal does not move, so he gets up and starts walking again, looking for a shellfish or a starfish, something alive. Children know how to circumvent death: they do not avoid it, but they go beyond it and always go a little further on.

Scrabble

*

Many years later, while leafing through the morning paper, I understood the meaning of the nickname that Amaboua had given me: "Toumaï."

On July 19, 2001, long after the events I have just reported here, an important scientific discovery took place in Tibesti, in the north of Chad. On that day, a seven-million-year-old skull was found in the Djourab desert. In the splendor of the dunes, an almost complete skull, two fragments of the lower jaw and three isolated teeth. This discovery led to the revelation of a new species, one of the first in the human line, the *Sahelanthropus tchadensis*, more commonly known as: Man of Toumaï. This fossil skull was given the name of Toumaï. In Goran, this word means "hope of life." In the Goran tradition, Toumaï is the name given to children born just before the dry season, because traditionally they had very little chance of survival.

Acknowledgments

The author warmly thanks the Fondation des Treilles, created by Anne Gruner Schlumberger, whose mission is, among other things, to open up and foster dialogue between the sciences and the arts in order to advance contemporary creation and research. It also welcomes researchers, writers, and photographic artists in the Treilles area (Var): www.les-treilles.com

Translator's Acknowledgment

Part of this work was done while I was a Fellow of the National Humanities Center, to which I express my gratitude.

Table of Illustrations

1. The child. The child always has a finger in his mouth. He gets to know the immense world of things by their flavor, but also by their texture and, so to speak, their complexion. Photo archive of Michaël Ferrier.

2. Map of Chad on a wall in Gorée.
Chad: a country closed like a gourd, without access to the sea, but also a plural and radiant territory, a wonder placed in the heart of Africa. Photo © Francesco Merlini / Prospekt Photographers.

3. Father and the guenon Babou, N'Djamena 1978.
"Only the old monkey knows how to peel the old peanut." (Massa Makan Diabaté, *Le boucher de Kouta*, 2002, Hatier éditions). Photo archive of Michaël Ferrier.

4. *The tree of creatures*, drawing in Indian ink and silver point by Raffi Kaiser, 2019.
The gnarled trunk, the effervescent foliage: it looked like a tree of a new species, giving birth to all kinds of animals, offering them shelter and crackling with joy. © Raffi Kaiser, 2019.

5. The boy with the dog, N'Djamena 1978.
It was the dogs that first taught me how to play and laugh. Live like a dog! Photo archive of Michaël Ferrier.

6. Child and dog on an unexploded bomb, Tigray, Ethiopia 1991. "When the powerful occupy the path, the weak goes into the bush with their good reason." (Ahmadou Kourouma, *En attendant le vote des bêtes sauvages*, 1998, Le Seuil). Photo © Dario Mitidieri / Getty-images.

7. On the banks of the Chari, February 11, 1979. I am a child of the river. The river teaches us the beat of the world, its incessant passage, its grace, and its entanglements. Photo archive of Michaël Ferrier.

8. Class of Collège Félix-Éboué, 1978-79. Dark, smooth skins like cumin oil next to pale, powdery skins like tapioca flour. Photo archive of Michaël Ferrier.

9. A Sara child wears scarifications in Chad around 1950-53. The incisions on his face, long and deep, give him a disconcerting appearance, as if he had cords carved in relief up to the top of the skull. Photo © Michel Huet / HOA-QUI—Gamma-Rapho.

10. Malik Sidibé, *Combat des amis avec pierres au bord du Niger*, 1976. They are there, mobile, happy, and learned, between dance and combat. Photo © Malick Sidibé / Courtesy of the MAGNIN-A Gallery, Paris.

11. *Le Tchad, pêche aux zemi*, drawing by Christian Seignobos from *Des Mondes Oubliés*, 2017. Canoes speak to me, they carry fish and traps, I myself ride the rivers again in my dreams and I bring back the spells of childhood in my nets. © Christian Seignobos / Éditions Parenthèses, 2017.

12. The child with the monkey. The animals, elegant, majestic, alive, give everything a touch of nobility. Photo archive of Michaël Ferrier.

13. Satellite map of N'Djamena. I am a son of N'Djamena: I like its shape, like a shell inclined to the curve of the river. Photo © Alamy photos / Photo12.

14. N'Djamena seen from the sky, in the 1970s, postcard, archives of the author.
N'Djamena: this outlying capital, this precarious but proud city, entirely arisen from the solitude of the sands.

15. Chad, *Joueur de balafon*, Leonard A. Lauder Postcard Archive, Museum of Fine Arts, Boston, Massachusetts / Bridgeman-images. © Michel Huet / Gamma Rapho.

16. *Griots des Gaws*, drawing by Christian Seignobos from *Des mondes oubliés*, 2017.
Agile intelligence, happiness of playing, joy of the balafon. © Christian Seignobos / Éditions Parenthèses, 2017.

17. Night in the bush, February 11, 1979. A childhood under the stars, by the Chari river, under the mosquito net. Photo archive of Michaël Ferrier.

18. The rooster. A rooster is a ball of feathers and muscles. Uncompromising and exuberant, tenacious as well as taciturn, the rooster opposes all those who approach this marvelous combination of violence and lightness. Photo © Francesco Merlini, Prospekt Photographers.

19. Passage of bomber planes over the house, N'Djamena, February 1979. Photo archives of Michaël Ferrier.

20. Oxen from the islands of Lake Chad, "Voyage au Congo" series by Marc Allégret and André Gide, February 1926. © RMN-Grand-Palais. Archives of the Catherine Gide Foundation.

21. Press clipping of February 14, 1978, Valentine's Day, author's records.

22. Raymond Depardon, *Tchad*, March 1980. Is there no other word for house? Has the word for patience already been burned? Has the word love succumbed to the gunfire? Because there it was clear and apparent: I had come to the end of my childhood. Photo © Raymond Depardon/Magnum Photos

Cover: lettering by Pierre Alechinsky. © *Mercure de France, 2019.*